REVIEWS FOR THE ROMANS ROAD

*In reading several days of devotions I have found the answer to the everlasting question; Yes, I'm really saved!!!!! I have been since 1995. I'm 77 years old. I know I have a long way to honor our Lord Jesus Christ. Of 24 devotions I've read I'm not even close. Jesus forgive me my short comings. I have read several Daily Devotionals, but "The Romans Road" gives a young or older Christian **all** the understanding and tools to enhance not only their own lives but more importantly the non-Christian in coming to be saved and to know how much they are **loved** by Jesus Christ. Get this book and find the real Jesus for your life. He is waiting; just call on his name, and he will answer. I give this one ★★★★★.*

RICHARD MOORE

The author accomplished what he set out to do: "equip the reader with the foundational doctrines of the Christian faith, and to deepen the reader's faith experiences."

*The reader will be enriched in his faith as he reads and applies **The Romans Road** devotional.*

TALMADGE BARNES

***The Romans Road** leads you through life's trails and shows that when you finally cry out to God for help, you will experience God grace, mercy, and freedom in Christ. This devotional is encouraging and comforting as you read it and grow in your relationship with God.*

HEATHER ALLEN

With the help of this book, I came to enjoy Romans more than ever. I particularly liked the writings focused on the grace of God. God's grace is so much greater than our human minds can conceive. We no longer must have the identity of a sinner. We get to trade that identity, and through Jesus become a child of God, dearly loved and important to Him. We no longer must seek the approval of human beings. With faith, we already have the approval of our Creator. It is through grace and faith that God produces the fruit He wants in our lives.

LIBBY WATSON, LPC

The Romans Road *is truly inspiring to read day by day. It teaches all believers God's Word and how to live as a follower of Jesus. It begins with directions of how to be saved, which is most important of all. After that it speaks well on how to live out your salvation. It's a very good read for anyone that would decide to read it!*

CAMERON BARNES

*When reading Dr. Jenkins' book **The Romans Road**, I immediately thought of how his life's passion is to share the saving love of Christ with those around him. Like Paul, he is so eager to preach the gospel! I couldn't help but think of a story Dr. Jenkins once told. He was riding around in the country and felt compelled to stop and pray at a church he had come upon. When entering, he was greeted by the church's custodian. He asked her if she knew Jesus as her Savior. She replied she did not. She had worked at that church for many years, and no one had ever asked her that question. Sharing the Roman's Road with her, she came to know the Lord that day. The word of God is powerful unto salvation, whether it's the first event of salvation or the power of bringing believers into a greater joy and presence of a holy God. I highly recommend **The Romans Road** whether you have questions about how to be rescued from your sins or you are already a follower of Jesus Christ.*

KARNE PARKISON

THE
ROMANS
ROAD

"Walking With Paul Through the Book of Romans"

A DAY-BY-DAY DEVOTIONAL

REVIVING THE CHURCH | REACHING THE LOST

JEHOVAH JIREH *Ministries*
THE LORD WHO PROVIDES

CONTENTS

THE
ROMANS
ROAD

ACKNOWLEDGMENTS AND DEDICATION

I would like thank God for the Jehovah Jireh Ministries Board of Directors. Without their advice, prayers, support, and holding this ministry accountable we simply could not do what we do in making Christ known to the world. They are truly godly men who put the Lord Jesus first in all they do.

This work on Romans are dedicated to the those men, our Board of Directors, who continually give their time, talents, treasures, prayers, and advice for the furthrance of the Gospel of our Lord Jesus.

ABOUT THE AUTHOR

Dr. Ralph Jenkins has been a Christian for 43 years and has served in full time ministry for 30 years. He has spent that time reading, studying, and memorizing God's word. He has often said, "People don't care what you know until they know that you care".

Dr. Jenkins has pastored four churches and is the founder of Jehovah Jireh Ministries (JJM). JJM has a mission to take the gospel to the world, holding crusades and revivals, training pastors, and planting churches among the unreached. He personal motto is Isaiah 6:8-9; *Then I heard the voice of the Lord saying, "Whom shall I send, who will go for us?" Then I said, "Here I am, Send me!"*

Dr. Jenkins has spent over 20 years traveling to Romania, Jamaica, UK, India, and Pakistan to proclaim the gospel to those who are perishing and to equip and encourage Christ's beloved church.

His wife Tammy is the heart of it all. Without God putting her in his life over 40 years ago there is no way he would be serving the Lord now. He has said, that without a doubt, he is one man that married the woman God ordained for him to have from the foundations of the earth. Christ is his first love and then Tammy. She is his wife, caretaker, secretary and most of all his #1 Prayer Warrior.

He has a daughter and son-in-law along with two grandchildren. They are also in full time ministry today pastoring God's church and assisting Ralph & Tammy with Jehovah Jireh Ministries.

PREFACE

Dear Reader:

Welcome to *The Romans Road* Daily Devotional.

This book is more than a collection of daily readings; it is an invitation to embark on a journey that will deepen your understanding of the Christian faith and your relationship with the Lord. The book of Romans is a treasure trove of doctrine, offering profound insights into the righteousness of God, the power of grace, and the incredible gift of salvation through Jesus Christ.

Our Purpose: The purpose of this devotional is simple: to equip you with the foundational doctrines of the Christian faith in a way that is engaging, encouraging, and enjoyable. Each day, you will walk through passages of Romans that have shaped the beliefs of countless believers over centuries. But more than just teaching you theology, I pray that these devotions will help you experience the joy of a daily, intimate walk with the Lord through His Word.

As you work through these pages, we hope you will discover the beauty and power of God's truth in new and exciting ways. Whether you're reading Romans for the first time or the hundredth time, there is always more to uncover, more to experience, and more to apply to your life.

Our Desire is that this devotional will not only to teach but inspire you in your walk with the Lord daily, strengthen your faith, and stir you up to live out the truth of God's word in your everyday journey. The doctrines of Romans are life-giving, transforming truths that lead to a deeper understanding of who God is and how He has calls His people to live and walk through this life with Him.

Our Walk: Let's walk this road together—one that leads to a greater faith, deeper joy, and a closer relationship with the One who made the way for us, Jesus, who is our Way Maker. As we walk with Him, we will discover that no one loves us like He does, no one has done more for us than Him, and no one desires to see walk through this victorious and triumphant more than Christ our Lord. His desire is for us to live a life a life filled with His blessing and favor, even the midst of trials of tribulations, throughout our life's journey.

God has a plan and purpose for us that in His Sovereignty, He planned and purposed from the foundations of the earth. All of this is in the book Romans.

I pray that you will enjoy this Daily Walk through Romans and more so, your daily walk with Jesus.

In Christ,
Dr. Ralph Jenkins
Jehovah Jireh Ministries

TO THE READER OF
"THE ROMANS ROAD"

First, I want to thank you for picking up this devotional book. I believe that God has something special to say to you through these pages. So, let's talk about how to get the most out of this devotional. Imagine we are right there with you, encouraging you as you hold this book in your hands.

TAKE YOUR TIME

Don't rush through the devotions. Each day is designed to be a moment of pause in your busy life, a time to connect with God and allow Him to speak to your heart. I encourage you to find a quiet place, free from distractions. Maybe it's first thing in the morning, during a lunch break, or before you go to bed. The important thing is that you make this time a priority. Give yourself permission to slow down and absorb what God is saying through His Word.

READ PRAYERFULLY

Before you start reading each devotion, take a moment to pray. Ask God to open your heart and mind to His Word. Pray for understanding and for the Holy Spirit to guide you as you read. This book is more than just words on a page; it's a tool for God to speak into your life. So approach it with an open heart and a prayerful attitude.

FOLLOW ALONG IN YOUR BIBLE

As you read each devotional, you'll find a scripture reading that goes along with it. I want to encourage you to open your Bible and read those passages yourself. There's something powerful about seeing God's word with your own eyes. Write down any thoughts, questions, or insights that come to mind. Don't worry if you don't understand everything right away. The Bible is a living book, and each time you read it, God can reveal new truths to you.

STUDY AND REFLECT

Each devotion is designed to dig a little deeper into the scripture and help you understand what it means and how it applies to your life. Take time to think about the questions or ideas presented. Reflect on how the message relates to your own experiences. Be honest with yourself and with God. If something challenges you, write it down. If a particular verse or idea stands out, highlight it.

APPLY WHAT YOU LEARN

The real transformation happens when we take what we've read and learned and apply it to our daily lives. At the end of each devotional, you'll find a challenge or practical step to take. Don't skip over this part: these challenges are meant to help you live out your faith in a tangible way. Whether it's spending more time in prayer, showing kindness to someone, or stepping out in faith, these actions are where growth happens.

COMMIT TO FOLLOW THROUGH

I know it can be easy to read a devotional, feel encouraged, and then move on without making any changes. I want to encourage you to commit to following through with the daily challenge. Let each devotion be a steppingstone in your journey of faith. God will honor your commitment and faithfulness, and you'll begin to see the fruits of your efforts in your spiritual growth and relationship with Him.

STAY ENCOURAGED

There may be days when you feel like you're not learning anything or when life gets so busy that finding time for devotions seems impossible. Remember, it's okay. God sees your heart and your efforts. Keep coming back to Him. Even if you miss a day or two, pick up right where you left off. The important thing is to keep moving forward, one step at a time.

WALKING FURTHER

At the end of each weeks devotionals, you will find several questions that relate to the prior week's set of devotions. They are designed to help you go further in your walk with Jesus. Please take the time to read and answer and allow the Holy Spirit to take you further into your faith than you may have gone before.

I'M PRAYING FOR YOU

Finally, I want you to know that we are praying for you as you go through this devotional. Our prayer is that God will use these devotions to strengthen your faith, deepen your understanding of His Word, and draw you closer to Him. We are standing with you in spirit, cheering you on, and believing that God is going to do amazing things in your life. We pray that each day's devotion will be just what you need for that day.

Thank you again for embarking on this journey with *The Romans Road*. We can't wait to see how God moves in your life as you read, follow, study, and apply His Word.

AM I SAVED???

It may be that as you start to read this devotional that you are unsure if you are or are not saved. Before you begin, may we present to you the gospel of Christ and how to be saved.

THE ROMAN ROAD TO SALVATION

SCRIPTURE READING:

- Romans 3:23 (NASB): "For all have sinned and fall short of the glory of God."
- Romans 6:23 (NASB): "For the wages of sin is death, but the gracious gift of God is eternal life in Christ Jesus our Lord."
- Romans 5:8 (NASB): "But God demonstrates His own love toward us, in that while we were still sinners, Christ died for us."
- Romans 10:9-10 (NASB): "That if you confess with your mouth Jesus as Lord, and believe in your heart that God raised Him from the dead, you will be saved; for with the heart a person believes, resulting in righteousness, and with the mouth he confesses, resulting in salvation."
- Romans 10:13 (NASB): "For everyone who calls on the name of the Lord will be saved."

DEVOTION:

The Romans Road to Salvation is a powerful and clear presentation of the gospel, drawn from key verses in the book of Romans. It walks us through the steps of recognizing our need for salvation, understanding God's solution, and responding to His offer of eternal life.

STEP 1: OUR CONDITION—ROMANS 3:23

The journey begins with a sobering truth: "For all have sinned and fall short of the glory of God." Every person is born into sin, and no one can measure up to God's perfect standard. This verse eliminates any illusion that we can earn our way to heaven or live a life good enough to merit God's favor. We must first acknowledge our sinful state, our inability to save ourselves.

STEP 2: THE CONSEQUENCE—ROMANS 6:23

Sin comes with a dire consequence: "For the wages of sin is death." Sin leads to spiritual death, a separation from God. But this verse doesn't end with despair; it presents hope: "But the gracious gift of God is eternal life in Christ Jesus our Lord." While our sin earns us death, God's grace offers us eternal life through Jesus. This gift is not something we can achieve; it's something we receive.

STEP 3: GOD'S DEMONSTRATION OF LOVE—ROMANS 5:8

God didn't wait for us to clean up our act. Romans 5:8 declares, "But God demonstrates His own love toward us, in that while we were still sinners, Christ died for us." Jesus' sacrificial death on the cross is the ultimate expression of God's love. He took our place, bore our punishment, and made a way for us to be reconciled with God.

STEP 4: OUR RESPONSE—ROMANS 10:9-10

Salvation requires a personal response: "If you confess with your mouth Jesus as Lord, and believe in your heart that God raised Him from the dead, you will be saved." This verse outlines the simplicity and depth of faith. It's not just intellectual assent; it's a heart-deep belief that transforms your life. Confessing Jesus as Lord means surrendering to His authority and trusting in His resurrection as the cornerstone of your faith.

STEP 5: ASSURANCE OF SALVATION—ROMANS 10:13

The journey concludes with a promise: "For everyone who calls on the name of the Lord will be saved." This is the assurance we have in Christ—no one who sincerely seeks Him will be turned away. God's offer of salvation is open to all, regardless of background, past sins, or present circumstances.

REFLECTION:

As you reflect on these verses, consider where you are on this journey. Have you acknowledged your need for salvation? Have you received God's gift of eternal life? If you've already walked this road, take time to thank God today for your salvation.

Ask Him: who in your life needs to hear the Gospel of Christ? The Romans Road is not just a path to personal salvation; it's a guide we can share with others who are seeking the truth. Just pass this message along to them.

If today you realize your need to be saved and can believe with all your heart that Jesus died for your sins and God raised Him from the dead then we invite you to say, from the heart, this prayer.

PRAYER:

Heavenly Father, I know I have sinned and come short of what you expect of me. I know I need salvation. Today, I confess Christ as my Lord. I believe Jesus died for my sins and rose from the grave. According to your holy Word, if I confess with my mouth and believe with my heart in Christ Jesus then I am saved. I thank you for saving me and I ask you to lead me now and help me live the life you have called me to. In Jesus Name, Amen.

If you prayed this prayer with all your heart and then according to God's word, you now saved. We praise God for your salvation.

Please, drop us a message at info@jehovahjirehministries.com and let us know of your decision. May God bless you as you begin *The Romans Road* daily devotional.

WEEK 1:
PAUL'S GREETING AND DESIRE TO VISIT ROME
(ROMANS 1:1-15)

CALLED TO BE AN APOSTLE
  – ROMANS 1:1

PROMISED THROUGH THE PROPHETS
  – ROMANS 1:2

THE SON OF GOD IN POWER
  – ROMANS 1:3-4

GRACE AND APOSTLESHIP ROMANS
  – ROMANS 1:5

BELONGING TO JESUS
  – ROMANS 1:6-7

LONGING TO ENCOURAGE ONE ANOTHER
  – ROMANS 1:8-12

EAGER TO PREACH THE GOSPEL
  – ROMANS 1:13-15

DAY 1: CALLED TO BE AN APOSTLE

Scripture Reading: Romans 1:1
Focus Verse: Romans 1:1 (NASB)
"Paul, a bond-servant of Christ Jesus, called as an
apostle, set apart for the gospel of God."

DEVOTION:

A young woman felt a deep calling on her heart to serve her local community. At first, she wasn't sure how or where to begin, and doubt often crept in. However, an opportunity arose through a small outreach group that ministered to homeless families. She joined, feeling it was just a small act, but soon her love for serving others grew into a passion that drove her entire life. She realized that her calling was much more than a single action; it was a life set apart for service.

Paul introduces himself to the Romans not by listing his accomplishments or qualifications but by stating two critical aspects of his identity: he is a bond-servant of Jesus Christ and an apostle, set apart for the gospel of God. His role as an apostle wasn't something he achieved through education or ambition, it was a divine calling, a mission that defined his life. This title, "bond-servant," or "slave," speaks of complete surrender and devotion to the will of his Master. For Paul, being set apart meant living every moment with the singular focus of spreading the gospel.

The question we must ask ourselves is, "What has God called me to?" Like Paul, each of us has been set apart for God's purpose. It may not always involve preaching from a pulpit or traveling across countries to spread the gospel, but it could be simple yet profound acts of service in our homes, workplaces, or communities. Understanding our calling starts with understanding who we belong to. When we realize we are first and foremost servants of Christ, our life's purpose takes shape.

Being set apart involves living a life different from the world's values, holding tightly to God's truth and reflecting Christ's love in our actions. Paul knew that the gospel was his life's purpose, and everything else flowed from that. In the same way, our purpose is defined by how we live out our relationship with Christ in everything we do.

FURTHER READING:

Galatians 1:15-16; Acts 9:15; 1 Corinthians 9:16-17; 2 Timothy 1:9

PRAYER

Lord, thank You for calling me to be Your servant. Help me to live a life that is set apart for the gospel, faithfully fulfilling the mission You have for me. Give me clarity about how I can serve You in my daily life and the courage to walk in that calling. Amen.

CHALLENGE

Today, take time to reflect on how God is calling you to serve. Whether it's something big or small, take one intentional step toward living out that calling. Surrender any doubts or fears and trust that God has a specific purpose for your life.

DAY 2: PROMISED THROUGH THE PROPHETS

Scripture Reading: Romans 1:2
Focus Verse: Romans 1:2 (NASB)
"Which He promised beforehand through
His prophets in the holy Scriptures."

DEVOTION

A man marveled at the way a book he had read years ago seemed to predict events that were unfolding in his life. But the book wasn't a secular work of fiction or a philosophical treatise—it was the Bible. Every prophecy, every promise spoken centuries ago was coming to life before his eyes, confirming once again the eternal truth of God's word.

In this verse, Paul grounds the gospel in the Old Testament, reminding the Roman believers that the gospel wasn't a new idea. God's plan to redeem humanity through His Son was foretold long ago through His prophets. The promises in the Old Testament—from Genesis to Malachi—find their fulfillment in Christ. From the *protoevangelium* in Genesis 3:15 to Isaiah's prophecies about the suffering servant (Isaiah 53), God was preparing His people for the arrival of the Messiah.

The fact that the gospel was "promised beforehand" through the prophets assures us of God's sovereignty and the reliability of His Word. God wasn't reacting to human failure with a last-minute plan, He had purposed to redeem us from the beginning. This gives us confidence that God's promises today are just as sure. We can trust that what He has spoken in His Word will come to pass, no matter how long it takes.

In a world where promises are often broken, God's promises are the anchor of our faith. They remind us that God is faithful to fulfill every word He has spoken, whether it's promises of peace, provision, or eternal life. We are part of a story that God has been writing for generations, and the fulfillment of prophecy through Jesus assures us that His promises to us are trustworthy.

FURTHER READING

Isaiah 53:3-6; Jeremiah 31:31-34; Luke 24:44; 2 Peter 1:19-21

PRAYER

Father, thank You for the promises You have given us in Scripture. Help me to stand on Your Word, trusting in the reliability of what You have spoken. Strengthen my faith as I wait for Your promises to unfold in my life. Amen.

CHALLENGE

Spend time reading a prophecy from the Old Testament that points to Jesus (e.g., Isaiah 53). Reflect on how this prophecy reveals God's faithfulness and plan to redeem His people.

DAY 3: THE SON OF GOD IN POWER

Scripture Reading: Romans 1:3-4
Focus Verse: Romans 1:4 (NASB)
"Who was declared the Son of God with power by the resurrection from the dead, according to
the Spirit of holiness, Jesus Christ our Lord."

DEVOTION

A man who had always struggled with doubt once shared that the resurrection of Jesus transformed his faith. He said, "I knew that if Jesus truly rose from the dead, then everything He said must be true." This realization changed his entire outlook on life and gave him a confidence in God that he had never experienced before.

In these verses Paul establishes the identity of Jesus Christ. While Jesus' birth fulfilled the promises of the prophets, it was His resurrection that powerfully declared Him to be the Son of God. The resurrection is not just an event—it is the cornerstone of our faith. It validates everything Jesus taught, His victory over sin, and His lordship over all.

The resurrection changes everything. It's more than a historical fact; it's the power that gives life to our faith. When we truly grasp the significance of the resurrection, it brings clarity and purpose to our lives. Jesus didn't just claim to be the Son of God—He proved it by rising from the dead. As believers, we must live in the power of the resurrection, understanding that it not only secures our eternal salvation but also empowers us to live victorious lives today.

The Spirit of holiness, mentioned in this verse, shows us that Jesus' resurrection is linked with the work of the Holy Spirit. The same Spirit that raised Christ from the dead is at work in us, giving us the power to overcome sin and live holy lives. Let's embrace this truth and walk in the fullness of the Spirit's power.

FURTHER READING
1 Corinthians 15:12-22; Philippians 2:9-11; Ephesians 1:19-21

PRAYER
Lord Jesus, thank You for the power of Your resurrection, which confirms that You are the Son of God. Help me to live in the victory and hope that Your resurrection brings and fill me with the power of Your Spirit to walk in holiness every day. Amen.

CHALLENGE
Reflect on the power of the resurrection. How does it shape your faith and your daily life? Take time today to praise God for the victory of Jesus over sin and death and share this truth with someone who may need to hear it.

DAY 4: GRACE AND APOSTLESHIP

Scripture Reading: Romans 1:5
Focus Verse: Romans 1:5 (NASB)
"Through whom we have received grace and apostleship to bring about the obedience of faith among all the Gentiles for His name's sake."

DEVOTION

A man who had once struggled with self-worth shared how he had come to realize that every opportunity he had to serve was a gift from God. "It's not about what I deserve or what I've earned," he said. "It's about God's grace allowing me to be a part of His plan." This changed his outlook on serving others. It became a privilege instead of a burden.

Paul recognizes that both his apostleship and the grace he received came from God. He didn't earn his role as an apostle through merit or personal ambition. Instead, he was chosen by grace to lead others to the obedience of faith. The purpose of this calling wasn't for personal glory, but for the name of Jesus to be honored among all nations. His mission was clear: to lead the Gentiles to faith in Christ.

As believers we are also recipients of God's grace. Like Paul we've been called to a life of service, not because of what we've done, but because of God's great love for us. Our lives are a testimony to His grace, and we are called to reflect that grace to others. This means our faith isn't just about receiving blessings for ourselves; it's about bringing others into a relationship with Jesus. Every opportunity we have to share the gospel, serve others, or demonstrate Christlike love is a gift of grace. Let's embrace this calling and live in a way that brings honor to His name.

FURTHER READING

Ephesians 3:7-8; 1 Corinthians 15:10; 2 Corinthians 4:15

PRAYER

Lord, thank You for the grace You've poured out in my life. Help me to walk in that grace, serving You and leading others to faith. May everything I do be for the sake of Your name and for Your glory. Amen.

CHALLENGE

Consider how you can use the grace God has given you to serve others this week. Whether it's sharing your faith or helping someone in need, remember that every act of service is for His name's sake.

DAY 5: BELONGING TO JESUS

Scripture Reading: Romans 1:6-7
Focus Verse: Romans 1:6 (NASB)
"Among whom you also are the called of Jesus Christ."

DEVOTION

A child adopted into a loving family once said, "I know I belong here. I was chosen." That deep sense of belonging changed the way she viewed herself and the world around her. Knowing she was wanted gave her a confidence and peace that she had never felt before.

Paul reminds the believers in Rome that they are "called of Jesus Christ." This is not just a generic statement—it's deeply personal. To be called by Jesus means that we are chosen, loved, and invited into a relationship with Him. It's a profound truth that shapes our identity as believers. We don't belong to this world or its values, we belong to Christ.

Belonging to Jesus changes everything about how we see ourselves. We are not defined by our past mistakes, our present struggles, or our future uncertainties. Our identity is rooted in the fact that we are called by Christ and belong to Him. This gives us confidence and purpose. No matter where life takes us, we can stand firm in the knowledge that we are loved and chosen by God.

Our belonging to Jesus also calls us to live differently. We are not to conform to the patterns of this world but to live in a way that reflects our identity in Christ. Let's embrace the freedom and joy that come from knowing we belong to Him, and let's live in a way that honors that calling.

FURTHER READING

John 15:16; 1 Peter 2:9-10; Ephesians 1:4-5

PRAYER

Father, thank You for calling me to belong to Jesus. Help me to live with confidence in my identity as Your child and to reflect that identity in everything I do. Amen.

CHALLENGE

Reflect on what it means to belong to Jesus. Let this truth shape your actions and mindset, and live with the confidence that you are loved, chosen, and called by Him.

DAY 6: LONGING TO ENCOURAGE ONE ANOTHER

Scripture Reading: Romans 1:8-12
Focus Verse: Romans 1:12 (NASB)
"That is, that I may be encouraged together with you while among you, each of us by
the other's faith, both yours and mine."

DEVOTION

In a small Bible study group, members regularly shared how God was working in their lives. One member commented, "Every time we meet, I leave feeling so encouraged. It's like each of us lifts the other up, and I'm reminded that I'm not walking this faith journey alone."

Paul expresses his longing to visit the Roman believers, not only to strengthen their faith but also to be encouraged by theirs. This mutual encouragement is one of the greatest gifts of Christian fellowship. When believers come together to share their faith, struggles, and victories, everyone benefits. Faith is contagious, and we are meant to strengthen one another in our walk with Christ.

Encouragement is a powerful tool in the Christian life. Just as Paul longed to be encouraged by the Roman believers, we too need the support and encouragement of fellow Christians. We're not meant to walk this journey alone. Sharing our faith stories, praying for one another, and offering words of support are vital ways to build each other up. Let's be intentional about seeking out opportunities to encourage others and to be encouraged by their faith in return.

FURTHER READING

1 Thessalonians 5:11; Hebrews 10:24-25; Ephesians 4:29

PRAYER

Lord, thank You for the gift of fellowship with other believers. Help me to be a source of encouragement to others, and may I be strengthened through their faith as well. Amen.

CHALLENGE

Reach out to someone today to offer encouragement. Whether it's through prayer, a kind word, or simply sharing your faith, take time to strengthen a fellow believer.

DAY 7: EAGER TO PREACH THE GOSPEL

Scripture Reading: Romans 1:13-15
Focus Verse: Romans 1:15 (NASB)
"So, for my part, I am eager to preach the gospel to you also who are in Rome."

DEVOTION

A young evangelist, passionate about sharing the gospel, once said, "I can't help but tell others about Jesus. It's the best news I've ever received!" His eagerness to share the message was contagious, inspiring others to do the same.

Paul expresses his eagerness to preach the gospel to the believers in Rome. His passion for sharing the good news wasn't just about duty—it was driven by a deep love for Christ and for those who needed to hear. Paul understood the transformative power of the gospel and wanted everyone to experience it. His eagerness serves as a model for all of us as we consider how we share the gospel with others.

When was the last time you were eager to share the gospel? Paul's enthusiasm reminds us of the urgency and importance of sharing the good news with those around us. The gospel isn't just something we believe, it's something we are called to proclaim. Whether through words, actions, or relationships, we are all tasked with making Christ known. Let's ask God to reignite our passion for sharing the gospel and to give us opportunities to speak truth into the lives of those around us.

FURTHER READING

Matthew 28:19-20; 1 Corinthians 9:16; 2 Timothy 4:2

PRAYER

Lord, stir in me a passion to share the gospel with others. Help me to see every opportunity as a chance to make Your name known and to bring others into a relationship with You. Amen.

CHALLENGE

This week, pray for opportunities to share the gospel. Ask God to give you boldness and wisdom in how to approach conversations, and trust Him to work through your willingness to proclaim His name.

WALKING FURTHER

1. What does it mean to be "set apart" for the gospel? How does this calling shape your daily life?

2. How do Old Testament prophecies about Jesus strengthen your confidence in God's word?

3. In what ways has the power of the resurrection impacted your life and faith? How can you live more fully in that power?

4. Reflect on your role as a recipient of God's grace. How does this shape your attitude toward sharing the gospel with others?

5. What does it mean to belong to Jesus? How does this identity influence your decisions and relationships?

6. How can you be more intentional about encouraging other believers in your life? What steps can you take to strengthen Christian fellowship?

7. How can you cultivate a deeper eagerness to share the gospel with others? What holds you back, and how can you overcome those barriers?

WEEK 2: THE GOSPEL OF CHRIST
(ROMANS 1:16-32)

THE POWER OF THE GOSPEL
 – ROMANS 1:16-17

GOD'S WRATH REVEALED
 – ROMANS 1:18-20

FOOLISHNESS OF IDOLATRY
 – ROMANS 1:21-23

GOD GAVE THEM OVER
 – ROMANS 1:24-25

THE CONSEQUENCES OF REJECTION
 – ROMANS 1:26-27

A DEPRAVED MIND
 – ROMANS 1:28-31

APPROVING WHAT IS EVIL
 – ROMANS 1:32

DAY 1: THE POWER OF THE GOSPEL

Scripture Reading: Romans 1:16-17
Focus Verse: Romans 1:16 (NASB)
"For I am not ashamed of the gospel, for it is the
power of God for salvation to everyone who believes, to the Jew first and also to the Greek."

DEVOTION

A young missionary once shared how, during her outreach in a foreign country, she was mocked for her faith. At first, she hesitated to speak
up, afraid of rejection. But then she remembered this verse and how the
gospel is the power of God for salvation. She realized that it wasn't about
how well she presented the message or how people responded. It was
about God's power working through the message of Christ. With renewed courage, she boldly shared the gospel, and many came to faith.

Paul's declaration that he is "not ashamed of the gospel" speaks to
the confidence and boldness we should have as followers of Christ. The
gospel isn't just a message of hope—it's the power of God for salvation.
This power isn't something we generate; it's God working through the
good news of Jesus' life, death, and resurrection. When we share the gospel, we are tapping into the very power that can change lives. We must
remember that our task is to proclaim the message; God does the work
of transformation.

No matter how the world views the gospel—whether with ridicule or
rejection—we must never be ashamed of it. The gospel has the power to
save all who believe, and it's a message that is worth sharing with boldness
and love. Let's embrace the power of the gospel in our own lives and trust
that God will use it to reach others.

FURTHER READING

1 Corinthians 1:18; 2 Timothy 1:8-10; Ephesians 2:8-9

PRAYER

Lord, thank You for the power of the gospel that brings salvation. Help me to never be ashamed of this message and to share it boldly with those around me. Strengthen my faith, and use me to bring others into Your Kingdom. Amen.

CHALLENGE

Think of someone in your life who needs to hear the gospel. Pray for an opportunity to share the good news with them, and trust in God's power to work through your words.

DAY 2: GOD'S WRATH REVEALED

Scripture Reading: Romans 1:18-20
Focus Verse: Romans 1:18 (NASB)
"For the wrath of God is revealed from heaven
against all ungodliness and unrighteousness of men
who suppress the truth in unrighteousness."

DEVOTION

A man who had lived a life of rebellion against God once shared how he had ignored the truth for years. He had heard about God's love and salvation but chose to suppress the truth because he didn't want to change his lifestyle. It wasn't until he faced the consequences of his choices that he began to understand the seriousness of God's judgment. This realization led him to repentance and ultimately to a relationship with Christ.

Paul's words in this passage may seem harsh, but they are a necessary reminder of God's holiness and justice. God's wrath is not a random display of anger—it is His righteous response to sin and rebellion. When people choose to reject God's truth and live in unrighteousness, they suppress the truth that has been made evident to them through creation and their own conscience.

The good news is that while God's wrath is real, His mercy is equally real. The gospel offers a way for us to be saved from His wrath through faith in Jesus Christ. As believers, we must hold onto the truth of both God's justice and His grace, recognizing that the gospel isn't just about love and forgiveness, it's also about salvation from the just consequences of sin. Let this sober reminder drive us to share the gospel with urgency.

FURTHER READING
Ephesians 5:6; John 3:36; Colossians 3:5-6

PRAYER

Lord, thank You for revealing the truth of Your justice and grace. Help me to live in the light of Your righteousness and to share the gospel with others, knowing that it offers salvation from the wrath to come. Amen.

CHALLENGE

Reflect on the seriousness of sin and God's judgment. Let this truth motivate you to share the gospel with those who have not yet turned to Christ.

DAY 3: FOOLISHNESS OF IDOLATRY

Scripture Reading: Romans 1:21-23
Focus Verse: Romans 1:21 (NASB)
"For even though they knew God, they did not honor
Him as God or give thanks, but they became futile in their
speculations, and their foolish heart was darkened."

DEVOTION

A man who had everything—success, money, and fame—once shared how empty his life felt. He had achieved all the things the world told him would bring happiness, but instead, he felt more lost and dissatisfied than ever before. It wasn't until he encountered Christ and turned away from the "idols" of success and wealth that he found true fulfillment.

Paul's description of humanity's descent into idolatry highlights the danger of turning away from God. Although people have knowledge of God, they often refuse to honor or thank Him, choosing instead to worship created things. Idolatry isn't just about bowing down to statues, it's about placing anything or anyone above God in our hearts. This could be money, success, relationships, or even our own self-interest.

When we prioritize anything over God, our hearts become darkened, and we lose the ability to see clearly. The more we turn away from God, the more we spiral into foolishness and emptiness. As believers, we must guard against the subtle idols in our lives, constantly refocusing our hearts on God and giving Him the honor and thanks He deserves.

FURTHER READING

Psalm 106:20-21; Isaiah 44:9-20; 1 John 5:21

PRAYER

Lord, help me to recognize any idols in my life and to turn my heart fully toward You. I want to honor You as the true and living God, giving You all the praise and thanks You deserve. Amen.

CHALLENGE

Take time to examine your life for any "idols," those things that may have taken God's rightful place. Surrender them to God and refocus your worship on Him alone.

DAY 4: GOD GAVE THEM OVER

Scripture Reading: Romans 1:24-25
Focus Verse: Romans 1:24 (NASB)
"Therefore God gave them over in the lusts
of their hearts to impurity, so that their bodies would be dishonored among them."

DEVOTION

A woman who had spent years trapped in destructive habits shared how she had once pushed God out of her life. Eventually, she reached a point where she felt utterly hopeless, having given herself over to things that she knew were wrong. But when she finally cried out to God for help, she experienced His mercy and found freedom in Christ.

Paul's sobering statement that "God gave them over" highlights the tragic consequences of persistent rebellion against God. When people continually reject God's truth and choose to follow their own desires, God eventually allows them to experience the full weight of their choices. This is not because God wants to harm them, but because He honors human free will. When we refuse to submit to God, we find ourselves enslaved to our own sinful desires.

However, even when God gives people over to their sinful choices, His mercy remains. He is always ready to forgive and restore anyone who turns back to Him in repentance. As believers, we must be vigilant in guarding our hearts against the deceitfulness of sin, knowing that God's desire is for us to live in freedom and purity.

FURTHER READING

Ephesians 4:19; Hosea 4:17; 2 Thessalonians 2:10-12

PRAYER

Father, help me to live a life that honors You. Keep my heart from being hardened by sin, and give me the strength to walk in purity and obedience to Your will. Amen.

CHALLENGE

Take time today to reflect on any areas of your life where you may have resisted God's truth. Ask Him to help you surrender fully to His will and to lead you in the path of righteousness.

DAY 5: THE CONSEQUENCES OF REJECTION

Scripture Reading: Romans 1:26-27
Focus Verse: Romans 1:26 (NASB)
"For this reason God gave them over to degrad-
ing passions; for their women exchanged the natural function for that which is unnatural."

DEVOTION

A counselor who worked with individuals struggling with addiction
once remarked, "When people reject what's healthy and right, they often
spiral into behaviors that harm them even more. The further they go
down that path, the harder it becomes to turn back." But she also shared
how hope remains for those who seek help and return to the right path.

In these verses, Paul continues to describe the downward spiral of sin
that occurs when people reject God's truth. As people persist in their rebellion, they engage in behaviors that not only dishonor their bodies but
also lead to deeper brokenness. This passage reminds us that sin always
has consequences, both in our relationship with God and in our personal
well-being.

While this passage speaks specifically of sexual sin, the principle applies to all forms of rebellion against God. Whenever we reject God's
design for our lives, we step into territory that leads to pain, confusion,
and harm. But the hope of the gospel is that no matter how far someone
has strayed, God's grace is always available to bring them back to whole-
ness in Christ.

FURTHER READING

1 Corinthians 6:9-11; Galatians 6:7-8; Hebrews 3:12-13

PRAYER

Lord, thank You for Your grace that covers even the darkest of sins. Help me to walk in obedience to Your truth, and give me the courage to share Your love with those who are struggling with the consequences of sin. Amen.

CHALLENGE

Consider someone you know who may be struggling with the consequences of sinful choices. Pray for them today, and look for an opportunity to share the hope of Christ with them.

DAY 6: A DEPRAVED MIND

Scripture Reading: Romans 1:28-31
Focus Verse: Romans 1:28 (NASB)
"And just as they did not see fit to acknowledge
God any longer, God gave them over to a depraved
mind, to do those things which are not proper."

DEVOTION

A man who had once been caught in a cycle of self-destructive behavior shared how his thinking had become so warped that he could no longer distinguish right from wrong. It wasn't until he encountered the truth of God's word that his mind began to heal, and he was able to see things clearly again.

When people persist in rejecting God, their minds become depraved, meaning their ability to think and reason properly is corrupted. This is why we see such brokenness and confusion in a world that has turned away from God. Without the light of God's truth, our minds are left in darkness, and we lose the ability to discern what is right.

As believers, we must be careful not to allow our minds to be influenced by the world's standards. Instead, we are called to renew our minds through the truth of God's word (Romans 12:2). Let's commit ourselves to daily soaking in Scripture and allowing the Holy Spirit to transform our thinking, so that we may walk in the light of His truth.

FURTHER READING

2 Timothy 3:8; Titus 1:15-16; Ephesians 4:17-18

PRAYER

Lord, renew my mind through Your Word. Keep me from the deceitfulness of sin, and help me to walk in the wisdom and truth that comes from knowing You. Amen.

CHALLENGE

Take time today to meditate on a passage of Scripture that challenges or encourages you. Ask God to use His Word to renew your thinking and help you see the world through His eyes.

DAY 7: APPROVING WHAT IS EVIL

Scripture Reading: Romans 1:32
Focus Verse: Romans 1:32 (NASB)
"And although they know the ordinance of God,
that those who practice such things are worthy of
death, they not only do the same, but also give
hearty approval to those who practice them."

DEVOTION

A woman who had been caught up in a destructive lifestyle shared how she had once surrounded herself with people who encouraged her bad choices. "We all knew what we were doing was wrong, but we cheered each other on. It wasn't until I hit rock bottom that I realized I needed to make a change."

One of the most dangerous aspects of sin is when people not only engage in evil but also celebrate it. This is what Paul describes in this verse: the approval and encouragement of sinful behavior. In today's culture, we see this often, where what is wrong is praised and what is right is ridiculed. As believers, we must stand firm in God's truth, even when the world around us approves of what is evil.

We are called to speak the truth in love, not to condemn, but to offer a better way—the way of Christ. Let's be a light in a dark world, refusing to approve of evil and instead pointing others to the life-changing truth of the gospel.

FURTHER READING

Isaiah 5:20; 2 Peter 2:1-3; 1 Timothy 4:1-2

PRAYER

Father, help me to stand firm in Your truth, even when the world around me approves of what is evil. Give me the courage to speak truth in love and to be a light in the darkness. Amen.

CHALLENGE

This week, be mindful of the influences in your life—whether media, friendships, or culture—that may subtly approve of what is evil. Ask God for discernment and commit to standing for His truth, even when it's unpopular.

WALKING FURTHER:
WEEK 2 QUESTIONS

1. What does it mean for the gospel to be "the power of God for salvation"? How does this truth impact the way you share the gospel with others?

2. How can we hold both the truth of God's wrath and His grace in balance? Why is it important to understand both aspects of God's character?

3. What are some modern "idols" that people (or even we as believers) may be tempted to place above God? How can we guard our hearts against idolatry?

4. Reflect on the phrase "God gave them over" in Romans 1:24-26. What does it mean for God to allow people to experience the consequences of their choices? How should this shape the way we approach people who are living in rebellion against God?

5. In what ways have you seen the consequences of rejecting God's truth in society today? How can you be a voice for truth and compassion in a world that approves of evil?

6. How can you ensure that your mind is being renewed daily by God's word? What practical steps can you take to guard your thinking from the influence of the world?

7. Paul describes a world that not only practices evil but also approves of those who do. How can we as Christians speak truth and live differently without falling into judgmentalism? How can we show love and offer hope to those who are trapped in sin?

WEEK 3: JUDGMENT AND RIGHTEOUSNESS
(ROMANS 2)

PASSING JUDGMENT
  – ROMANS 2:1-2

GOD'S KINDNESS AND REPENTANCE
  – ROMANS 2:3-4

STORING UP WRATH
  – ROMANS 2:5-6

GOD'S RIGHTEOUS JUDGMENT
  – ROMANS 2:7-8

NO PARTIALITY WITH GOD
  – ROMANS 2:9-11

THE LAW WRITTEN ON HEARTS
  – ROMANS 2:12-15

THE DAY OF JUDGMENT
  – ROMANS 2:16

DAY 1: PASSING JUDGMENT

Scripture Reading: Romans 2:1-2
Focus Verse: Romans 2:1 (NASB)
"Therefore you have no excuse, everyone who passes judgment, for in that which you judge another, you condemn yourself; for you who judge practice the same things."

DEVOTION

A man who had always been quick to point out the faults in others realized, during a conversation with a close friend, that he had been blind to his own shortcomings. His friend kindly pointed out, "You're so focused on judging others that you've forgotten to look in the mirror." That simple statement made him rethink his attitude and approach, leading him to ask for God's help in being more humble and gracious.

Paul's warning in Romans 2:1 is a reminder that none of us are above judgment. It's easy to see the flaws and sins of others, but often, we fail to acknowledge our own. Jesus spoke about this in the Sermon on the Mount when He cautioned against trying to remove the speck from someone else's eye while ignoring the log in our own (Matthew 7:1-5). This doesn't mean we ignore sin, but it does mean we should approach others with humility, recognizing that we too are in need of God's grace.

Passing judgment without examining ourselves first leads to hypocrisy. The same judgment we apply to others will be applied to us. Rather than condemning, we should extend grace, knowing that we are all sinners saved by the mercy of God.

FURTHER READING

Matthew 7:1-5; James 2:13; Luke 6:37

PRAYER

Lord, help me to see others with the same grace and mercy that You show me. Guard my heart against hypocrisy and teach me to approach others with humility and love, knowing that I am in need of Your grace every day. Amen.

CHALLENGE

This week, make an intentional effort to stop judging others. Whenever you feel tempted to criticize, take a moment to examine your own heart and extend grace instead.

DAY 2: GOD'S KINDNESS AND REPENTANCE

Scripture Reading: Romans 2:3-4
Focus Verse: Romans 2:4 (NASB)
"Or do you think lightly of the riches of His kindness and tolerance and patience, not knowing that the kindness of God leads you to repentance?"

DEVOTION

A woman struggling with addiction shared her story about how, for years, she had pushed away the idea of repentance. She thought she was too far gone, beyond help. It wasn't until she encountered the overwhelming kindness and love of God through a Christian recovery group that her heart softened. "It wasn't judgment or condemnation that changed me," she said, "it was the kindness of God that broke through my defenses."

Paul emphasizes that it is God's kindness, not His wrath, that leads us to repentance. The world often pictures God as harsh and condemning, but Scripture reveals that God is patient, kind, and merciful. He gives us time to turn to Him, not because He's indifferent to sin, but because He desires that none should perish (2 Peter 3:9). When we truly understand the depth of God's kindness, it moves us to turn from sin and toward Him.

Repentance is not just about feeling bad for our sins, it's a complete change of mind and heart. God's kindness should inspire us to change, not out of fear, but out of gratitude for His grace. Let's never take lightly the patience and kindness God has shown us and always remember that He is calling us to repentance through His love.

FURTHER READING

Titus 3:4-5; 2 Peter 3:9; Joel 2:13

PRAYER

Father, thank You for Your kindness and patience toward me. Help me to respond to Your love with a heart of repentance and a desire to live in a way that honors You. Amen.

CHALLENGE

Reflect on the ways God has shown kindness and patience in your life. Ask Him to help you cultivate a heart of repentance in response to His love and share His kindness with others.

DAY 3: STORING UP WRATH

Scripture Reading: Romans 2:5-6
Focus Verse: Romans 2:5 (NASB)
"But because of your stubbornness and unrepentant heart,
you are storing up wrath for yourself in the day of wrath
and revelation of the righteous judgment of God."

DEVOTION

A man was once known for his stubbornness and refusal to change his ways, even when it was clear that his decisions were leading to trouble. After years of bad choices, the consequences of his actions finally caught up with him. He described it as though every wrong decision had been accumulating, waiting to come crashing down. He realized too late that his stubbornness had only made things worse.

Paul warns that a stubborn and unrepentant heart doesn't just lead to trouble, it stores up God's wrath for the future. When we refuse to turn to God, we are essentially accumulating judgment for ourselves. This doesn't mean God is eager to punish; rather, it means that His righteous judgment will eventually come if we persist in our rebellion.

It's important to recognize that every moment we reject God's call to repentance, we're choosing to live outside of His grace. But it's never too late to turn back to God. His desire is that we come to Him in humility and repentance before the day of judgment arrives. Let's not wait until it's too late, but instead, let's respond to God's call with open hearts and willing spirits.

FURTHER READING

Psalm 95:7-8; Ezekiel 18:30-32; Hebrews 3:7-8

PRAYER

Lord, soften my heart and help me to turn away from stubbornness and sin. I don't want to store up wrath for myself. Instead, I want to live in the light of Your grace and righteousness. Amen.

CHALLENGE

Examine your heart today. Are there any areas where you've been stubborn or resistant to God's leading? Ask Him to help you surrender fully to His will.

DAY 4: GOD'S RIGHTEOUS JUDGMENT

Scripture Reading: Romans 2:7-8
Focus Verse: Romans 2:7 (NASB)
"To those who by perseverance in doing good seek for
glory and honor and immortality, eternal life."

DEVOTION

A woman who had been through many trials in her life once said, "I used to wonder if doing good even mattered, especially when life seemed so unfair. But then I realized that God sees everything, and He is just. I may not see the rewards now, but I know they're coming." Her perseverance, even in the face of difficulty, was rooted in her faith in God's righteous judgment.

Paul contrasts those who seek God's glory, honor, and immortality with those who are self-seeking and reject the truth. God's righteous judgment isn't just about punishing evil, it's also about rewarding those who faithfully follow Him. Our perseverance in doing good, even when it's hard, reflects our trust in God's ultimate justice.

As believers, we are called to pursue what is eternal, not what is temporary. We may not always see the rewards of our faithfulness in this life, but God promises eternal life to those who seek His glory and honor. Let's be encouraged to continue doing good, knowing that God's judgment is righteous and He will reward those who remain faithful.

FURTHER READING

Galatians 6:9; 1 Corinthians 9:24-25; 2 Timothy 4:7-8

PRAYER

Lord, help me to persevere in doing good, even when it's hard or when I don't see immediate results. I trust in Your righteous judgment and look forward to the reward of eternal life. Amen.

CHALLENGE

Today, choose to do good even when it's difficult. Trust that God sees your efforts and will reward your faithfulness in His perfect timing.

DAY 5: NO PARTIALITY WITH GOD

Scripture Reading: Romans 2:9-11
Focus Verse: Romans 2:11 (NASB)
"For there is no partiality with God."

DEVOTION

A young man who had always struggled with the idea of fairness was amazed when he learned that God doesn't show favoritism. In school, he often felt overlooked or left out. But when he discovered that God sees every person equally, without preference for status, wealth, or background, it brought him peace. "God doesn't judge by what the world values," he said, "He looks at the heart."

In a world filled with favoritism, where people are often judged by their appearance, success, or social standing, Paul's statement that "there is no partiality with God" is a powerful reminder. God doesn't judge based on external factors, He judges righteously and fairly. Whether Jew or Gentile, rich or poor, male or female, God's standard is the same for all: His truth, His justice, and His grace.

This truth should comfort us, knowing that God sees and values us, not because of our accomplishments, but because of who we are in Christ. It should also challenge us to avoid favoritism in our own relationships, treating others with the same fairness and love that God extends to all. In God's eyes, all people are equally in need of His grace, and all are equally able to receive it through Christ.

FURTHER READING

James 2:1-4; Acts 10:34-35; Galatians 3:28

PRAYER

Lord, thank You for being a just and impartial God. Help me to see others the way You see them, without favoritism, and to love and treat all people with the same grace You have shown me. Amen.

CHALLENGE

Reflect on any areas where you may show favoritism in your relationships. Ask God to help you treat others with the same fairness and love that He shows, regardless of their status or background.

DAY 6: THE LAW WRITTEN ON HEARTS

Scripture Reading: Romans 2:12-15
Focus Verse: Romans 2:15 (NASB)
"In that they show the work of the Law written in their hearts, their conscience bearing witness and their thoughts alternately accusing or else defending them."

DEVOTION

A woman who had never heard of the Bible shared how, deep down, she always felt a sense of right and wrong. Even though she wasn't raised in a religious environment, there were certain moral standards she naturally adhered to. "I guess it's just part of being human," she said. "There's something inside all of us that knows what's right and what's wrong."

Paul explains that even those who don't have the written law of Moses still have an internal sense of morality—God's law written on their hearts. This inner conscience bears witness to the fact that every person, regardless of culture or religion, has a built-in awareness of right and wrong. While this doesn't mean they are saved apart from Christ, it does mean that God's moral law is universally recognized.

For us as believers, this truth reminds us that God's standards are not arbitrary, they are woven into the very fabric of human existence. It also highlights the importance of the Holy Spirit's work in guiding and convicting us, helping us to live in alignment with God's truth. Let's be mindful of the ways God speaks to our hearts and consciences, leading us toward righteousness.

FURTHER READING

Jeremiah 31:33; Hebrews 10:16; Proverbs 20:27

PRAYER

Lord, thank You for writing Your law on my heart and for guiding me through Your Holy Spirit. Help me to listen to Your voice, to follow my conscience, and to live according to Your truth. Amen.

CHALLENGE

This week, pay close attention to the promptings of your conscience. Ask the Holy Spirit to guide you in making decisions that align with God's truth.

DAY 7: THE DAY OF JUDGMENT

Scripture Reading: Romans 2:16
Focus Verse: Romans 2:16 (NASB)
"On the day when, according to my gospel, God will
judge the secrets of men through Christ Jesus."

DEVOTION

A young man once shared how he had lived much of his life trying to hide his mistakes and sins from others. On the outside, he appeared successful and put together, but inside, he was full of guilt and shame. When he finally encountered Christ, he realized that nothing is hidden from God, and that true freedom comes from confessing and being forgiven.

Paul reminds us that there will be a day of judgment, where God will judge not only outward actions but also the hidden secrets of the heart. While this may seem intimidating, for believers, it's also a reminder that we are fully known by God—and fully loved. Christ's work on the cross means that we can approach the day of judgment with confidence, knowing that we are forgiven and clothed in His righteousness.

This truth should motivate us to live lives of integrity, not only in the things others can see but also in the thoughts and desires of our hearts. Let's continually surrender every part of ourselves to God, trusting that He will bring us into His eternal presence, not based on our perfection, but on Christ's perfect work on our behalf.

FURTHER READING

Hebrews 4:12-13; 2 Corinthians 5:10; 1 Peter 4:5

PRAYER

Lord, I thank You that I can stand before You with confidence because of what Christ has done. Help me to live a life of integrity, knowing that nothing is hidden from You. Search my heart and lead me in Your ways. Amen.

CHALLENGE

Take time to reflect on the "hidden" parts of your life—the thoughts, attitudes, or habits that may not be visible to others. Surrender these areas to God, and trust Him to bring healing, forgiveness, and transformation.

WALKING FURTHER:
WEEK 3 QUESTIONS

1. What does Paul mean when he says we condemn ourselves when we pass judgment on others (Romans 2:1)? How does this challenge your view of judging others?

2. How has God's kindness led you to repentance? In what ways can you extend that same kindness to others who may be struggling with sin?

3. What does Paul's warning about storing up wrath teach us about the consequences of stubbornness and unrepentance? How can we guard our hearts against these attitudes?

4. How does God's impartiality challenge the way we view and treat others? Are there any areas in your life where you struggle with favoritism or bias?

5. What does it mean to have God's law written on our hearts? How can we be more sensitive to the prompting of our conscience and the Holy Spirit in our daily lives?

6. How does the knowledge of a future judgment impact the way you live now? In what areas of your life do you need to bring more integrity and surrender to God?

7. How can we live in the balance of knowing that God sees everything, yet we are fully loved and forgiven in Christ? How does this truth affect your relationship with God and others?

WEEK 4:
THE LAW AND THE HEART
(ROMANS 2:17-3:8)

TEACHERS OF THE LAW
- ROMANS 2:17-20

PRACTICE WHAT YOU PREACH
- ROMANS 2:21-23

GOD'S NAME BLASPHEMED
- ROMANS 2:24

TRUE CIRCUMCISION
- ROMANS 2:25-29

THE ADVANTAGE OF THE JEW
- ROMANS 3:1-2

GOD'S FAITHFULNESS
- ROMANS 3:3-4

THE RIGHTEOUSNESS OF GOD
- ROMANS 3:5-8

DAY 1: TEACHERS OF THE LAW

Scripture Reading: Romans 2:17-20
Focus Verse: Romans 2:17 (NASB)
"But if you bear the name 'Jew' and rely
upon the Law and boast in God..."

DEVOTION

A well-educated Bible teacher was known for his knowledge of Scripture. He often taught others and was respected in the community. However, one day a friend gently asked, "You know the Scriptures so well, but do you live them?" This question pierced his heart, causing him to reflect on how much of what he taught was actually reflected in his own life. It was a humbling realization that knowledge without practice is empty.

Paul addresses the Jews who took pride in their knowledge of the Law, but he challenges them: does simply knowing the Law make you righteous? Being a teacher of God's word carries great responsibility, not only to teach correctly but to live out what we know. The true test of our relationship with God is not in how much Scripture we can recite or how well we can teach, but in how much we live out the truth we know.

Knowledge without transformation is useless. Whether we are teachers, pastors, or simply believers who know God's word, the challenge is to align our lives with what we teach and believe. Let's strive to be both hearers and doers of the Word, living out the gospel daily.

FURTHER READING

James 1:22-25; Matthew 7:24-27; 1 Timothy 4:16

PRAYER

Lord, help me not to rely on knowledge alone, but to live in obedience to Your Word. May my life reflect the truth of Your gospel in every area. Amen.

CHALLENGE

This week, reflect on how well your life aligns with what you know of Scripture. Are there areas where you're more focused on knowledge than obedience? Take a step to live out the truth you know.

DAY 2: PRACTICE WHAT YOU PREACH

Scripture Reading: Romans 2:21-23
Focus Verse: Romans 2:21 (NASB)
"You, therefore, who teach another, do you not teach yourself?"

DEVOTION

A man who regularly gave advice to others about maintaining integrity at work was caught in a scandal himself for cutting corners and falsifying reports. When confronted, he realized how much he had failed to practice what he preached. This hypocrisy not only damaged his reputation but also his ability to witness to others about his faith.

Paul's question cuts to the heart of hypocrisy: "You who teach others, do you not teach yourself?" It's easy to tell others how they should live, but far harder to live by those same standards. Whether in our personal relationships, workplaces, or ministries, our actions should reflect the truth we proclaim. Hypocrisy not only undermines our credibility but also damages the witness of the gospel.

We are called to practice what we preach, to live lives of integrity and consistency. When we teach others about the truths of God's word, we must hold ourselves accountable to those same truths. Let's be mindful that our lives are a living testimony of the gospel we proclaim.

FURTHER READING

Matthew 23:1-3; Titus 2:7-8; Luke 6:41-42

PRAYER

Lord, help me to live with integrity and consistency, practicing what I preach. May my life reflect Your truth and honor You in every area. Amen.

CHALLENGE

Examine areas where you might be instructing others but not living by those same standards. Ask God to help you align your life with His truth.

DAY 3: GOD'S NAME BLASPHEMED

Scripture Reading: Romans 2:24
Focus Verse: Romans 2:24 (NASB)
"For 'the name of God is blasphemed among the
Gentiles because of you,' just as it is written."

DEVOTION

A woman once told a story about how she had been turned away from church because of how Christians she knew treated others. "If that's what following Jesus looks like, I want nothing to do with it," she said. Their actions had pushed her further from God instead of drawing her closer. It took many years before she encountered a believer whose life reflected Christ in a way that drew her back to Him.

Paul's warning is sobering. Our actions can either glorify God or cause His name to be blasphemed. The Jews prided themselves on their knowledge of the Law, but their disobedience caused Gentiles to speak ill of God. As believers, we must be aware that our lives are a reflection of Christ to the world around us. When we live in a way that contradicts the gospel, we not only damage our witness but also dishonor God's name.

Our lives are meant to draw people to Christ, not push them away. Let's strive to live in a way that honors God in all we do, so that His name is glorified and not blasphemed because of our actions.

FURTHER READING

Ezekiel 36:22; Matthew 5:16; 1 Peter 2:12

PRAYER

Father, help me to live in a way that honors Your name. Forgive me for any actions that may have caused others to stumble and help me to reflect Christ in all I do. Amen.

CHALLENGE

Think about how your actions might be reflecting Christ to others. Are there areas where your witness could be causing others to misunderstand God's character? Ask God for wisdom and guidance in these areas.

DAY 4: TRUE CIRCUMCISION

Scripture Reading: Romans 2:25-29
Focus Verse: Romans 2:29 (NASB)
"But he is a Jew who is one inwardly; and circumcision is
that which is of the heart, by the Spirit, not by the letter."

DEVOTION

A pastor once shared a story about how he had grown up thinking
that being a Christian was about going to church, following the rules,
and checking off religious boxes. It wasn't until he had a personal encounter with Jesus that he realized faith is about transformation of the heart,
not outward ritual. "I was following religion, but not really following
Christ," he admitted.

Paul explains that true circumcision isn't about an external ritual but
about a heart transformed by the Spirit. Just as physical circumcision
marked the Jews as God's covenant people, the inward work of the Holy
Spirit marks believers as God's children. It's not enough to perform religious rituals or follow the rules outwardly; God is concerned with the
state of our hearts.

As Christians, we must ask ourselves: Is my faith just an outward
show, or is it rooted in a deep, internal transformation? True faith is
about being changed from the inside out, allowing the Holy Spirit to
renew our hearts and lives.

FURTHER READING

Deuteronomy 10:16; Colossians 2:11; Galatians 6:15

PRAYER

Lord, I want my faith to be more than just outward appearances.
Transform my heart by Your Spirit and help me to live in true relationship with You. Amen.

CHALLENGE

This week, reflect on your relationship with God. Are there areas where your faith has become more about external ritual than internal transformation? Ask the Holy Spirit to renew your heart.

DAY 5: THE ADVANTAGE OF THE JEW

Scripture Reading: Romans 3:1-2
Focus Verse: Romans 3:2 (NASB)
"Great in every respect. First of all, that they
were entrusted with the oracles of God."

DEVOTION

A man who had grown up in a Christian home reflected on how he used to take his upbringing for granted. "I had access to the Bible and Christian teaching my whole life, but I didn't realize what a privilege it was until much later. There are people around the world who would give anything to have the resources I had."

Paul asks an important question: If both Jews and Gentiles are equally under sin, what advantage do the Jews have? His answer is that the Jews were entrusted with the "oracles of God," God's word. They had the privilege of knowing God's law, His promises, and His plan of salvation. This was a tremendous advantage, yet it also came with great responsibility.

As Christians, we too are entrusted with the Word of God. We have access to the Scriptures, the teachings of Jesus, and the gospel message. But having access to the truth isn't enough; we must live by it. Let's not take for granted the privilege of knowing God's word. Instead, let's embrace it fully and live according to its teachings.

FURTHER READING

Deuteronomy 4:7-8; Psalm 147:19-20; Luke 12:48

PRAYER

Father, thank You for the privilege of knowing Your Word. Help me to treasure it and live according to its truth. May I never take for granted the gift of Your revelation. Amen.

CHALLENGE

This week, reflect on the privilege of having access to God's word. How are you using this privilege to grow in your faith and share the gospel with others?

DAY 6: GOD'S FAITHFULNESS

Scripture Reading: Romans 3:3-4
Focus Verse: Romans 3:3 (NASB)
"What then? If some did not believe, their unbelief
will not nullify the faithfulness of God, will it?"

DEVOTION

A woman shared how she had prayed for years for her husband to come to faith. She often grew discouraged and wondered if God had given up on him. But through the encouragement of friends and the truth of Scripture, she was reminded that even in the face of unbelief, God's faithfulness never wavers. "God is faithful, even when we doubt," she said. "I can trust Him to be true to His promises."

Paul addresses a concern here: If some of the Jews were unfaithful to God's covenant, does that mean God's promises are invalid? His answer is a resounding no. God's faithfulness is not dependent on human belief or unbelief. Even when we are faithless, God remains faithful. His character and promises are unchanging.

This is a comforting truth for all of us. There may be times when we fall short, doubt, or struggle in our faith, but God's faithfulness never changes. His promises stand firm, and His love endures forever. Let's rest in the assurance that God is faithful to complete what He has begun in us, regardless of our own shortcomings.

FURTHER READING

2 Timothy 2:13; Numbers 23:19; Lamentations 3:22-23

PRAYER

Lord, thank You for Your faithfulness, even when I fall short. Help me to trust in Your unchanging character and to rely on Your promises, knowing that You are always true to Your Word. Amen.

CHALLENGE

Reflect on areas in your life where you've struggled with doubt or unbelief. Surrender those areas to God, and trust in His faithfulness to fulfill His promises.

DAY 7: THE RIGHTEOUSNESS OF GOD

Scripture Reading: Romans 3:5-8
Focus Verse: Romans 3:5 (NASB)

"But if our unrighteousness demonstrates the righteousness of God, what shall we say? The God who inflicts wrath is not unrighteous, is He? (I am speaking in human terms.)"

DEVOTION

A young believer once struggled with the idea of God's judgment. "How can a loving God also inflict wrath?" she asked. It wasn't until her pastor explained that God's righteousness demands justice for sin that she began to understand. "God's wrath isn't a contradiction to His love," he explained. "It's a reflection of His holiness and justice."

In this passage, Paul addresses a common question: If human sin reveals the righteousness of God, does that mean God is unrighteous for judging sin? Paul's answer is clear: God is perfectly righteous, and His judgment of sin is just. God's holiness and righteousness demand that sin be dealt with. His wrath against sin is not a contradiction to His love but a necessary expression of His justice.

God's righteousness is both the source of our salvation and the standard by which He judges. Through Christ, God's righteousness is revealed, and we are justified by faith. But we must never forget that God's righteousness also means He will judge sin. Let's live in awe of His holiness, grateful for the grace we have received through Christ.

FURTHER READING

Romans 9:14-16; Psalm 51:4; Isaiah 45:21

PRAYER

Father, thank You for Your righteousness and justice. Help me to live in reverence of Your holiness and to trust in Your perfect judgment. Thank You for the grace I have received through Jesus Christ. Amen.

CHALLENGE

Reflect on the balance between God's righteousness and His grace. How can you live in a way that honors His holiness while embracing the grace He offers through Christ?

WALKING FURTHER:
WEEK 4 QUESTIONS

1. What does it mean to be a teacher of the law or a bearer of God's word today? How can we ensure that we are not just hearers but also doers of the Word?

2. In what areas of your life do you need to "practice what you preach"? How can you hold yourself accountable to living by the truth you proclaim?

3. How can our actions cause God's name to be blasphemed or honored? What steps can you take to ensure that your life reflects God's character and brings Him glory?

4. What does it mean for circumcision to be of the heart? How can we cultivate a heart that is truly transformed by the Spirit, rather than relying on external religious practices?

5. What does it mean to be entrusted with God's word? How can we ensure that we are faithful stewards of the truth we have been given?

6. How does God's faithfulness encourage you in times of doubt or difficulty? How can you trust in His promises even when circumstances seem uncertain?

7. How does understanding God's righteousness and justice affect the way you view sin and grace? How can you live in a way that reflects both the holiness of God and the grace of the gospel?

WEEK 5:
ALL ARE UNDER SIN
(ROMANS 3:9-31)

NONE IS RIGHTEOUS
   – ROMANS 3:9-12

THE POISON OF SIN
   – ROMANS 3:13-14

THE PATH OF PEACE
   – ROMANS 3:15-18

ACCOUNTABILITY TO GOD
   – ROMANS 3:19-20

JUSTIFIED BY FAITH
   – ROMANS 3:21-24

REDEMPTION IN CHRIST
   – ROMANS 3:25-26

BOASTING EXCLUDED
   – ROMANS 3:27-31

DAY 1: NONE IS RIGHTEOUS

Scripture Reading: Romans 3:9-12
Focus Verse: Romans 3:10 (NASB)
"As it is written, 'There is none righteous, not even one.'"

DEVOTION

Growing up, a young man prided himself on being "better" than others. He didn't get into trouble, went to church every Sunday, and lived a life that most would call "good." One day, during a Bible study, the group read Romans 3:10: "There is none righteous, not even one." The words hit him like a ton of bricks. He realized that while he had been comparing himself to others, he was missing the true standard—God's holiness. He shared with the group, "I thought I was righteous because I wasn't like others, but I forgot that righteousness is not about being better than people, but being right with God."

Paul's declaration in Romans 3:9-12 levels the playing field: no one is righteous on their own. It doesn't matter how morally upright we appear to others or how many good deeds we perform. When compared to God's perfect standard of holiness, we all fall short. The passage forces us to confront the uncomfortable truth that we cannot achieve righteousness through our own efforts.

This realization is essential to understanding the gospel. Until we recognize our need for a Savior, we will continue trying to earn righteousness through human means, which is impossible. Paul quotes from the Psalms and other Scriptures to show that this has always been God's message: all of humanity is in desperate need of grace. The good news is that while none of us are righteous on our own, Christ provides the righteousness we could never achieve.

This truth humbles us and reminds us of our deep need for grace. Let's stop striving to appear righteous in the eyes of others and instead embrace the righteousness offered to us through Christ. It's not about being better than those around us; it's about being made new through Jesus.

FURTHER READING
Psalm 14:1-3; Ecclesiastes 7:20; Isaiah 64:6

PRAYER
Lord, I acknowledge that I cannot be righteous on my own. Thank You for providing the righteousness I need through Jesus Christ. Help me to stop striving for approval from others and to rest in Your grace. Amen.

CHALLENGE
Take time this week to reflect on your own need for Christ's righteousness. Are there areas where you've been relying on your own efforts or comparing yourself to others? Surrender those areas to God, and trust in His provision.

DAY 2: THE POISON OF SIN

Scripture Reading: Romans 3:13-14
Focus Verse: Romans 3:13 (NASB)
"'Their throat is an open grave, with their tongues they
keep deceiving,' the poison of asps is under their lips."

DEVOTION

A man who had built his career on climbing the corporate ladder at
any cost found himself estranged from friends, colleagues, and even family. His ambition led him to manipulate situations and spread false rumors about those who stood in his way. Eventually, his actions caught up
with him, and he lost his job and his reputation. He later reflected, "My
words were like poison. They destroyed everything in my life, including
the trust of those closest to me. I didn't realize how toxic my words were
until the damage was already done."

Paul uses strong imagery here to describe the power of sin, particularly in our speech. Sin doesn't just reside in our actions but also in our
words, which have the ability to wound and destroy. "Their throat is an
open grave" paints a vivid picture of the death and decay that comes from
sinful speech. Whether through lies, gossip, slander, or deceit, our words
can be like poison, spreading harm to those around us.

As believers, we are called to speak words of life, not death. The
tongue has the power to build up or tear down, and as followers of
Christ, we must be intentional about using our words to reflect His love
and truth. This passage reminds us to examine our hearts, for our words
are a reflection of what's inside. If our hearts are filled with bitterness,
anger, or deceit, that will come out in our speech.

Let's be mindful of the power of our words, asking God to cleanse
our hearts so that our speech brings healing and encouragement rather
than harm. We may not always realize the weight of our words, but they
have the power to impact lives for good or for ill.

FURTHER READING

James 3:5-10; Proverbs 18:21; Matthew 12:36-37

PRAYER

Father, help me to recognize the power of my words. Cleanse my heart so that my speech reflects Your truth and love. Keep me from using words that wound and destroy and teach me to speak life to those around me. Amen.

CHALLENGE

Pay attention to your speech this week. Are your words bringing life or death? Ask God to help you use your words to build up others and bring healing, not harm.

DAY 3: THE PATH OF PEACE

Scripture Reading: Romans 3:15-18
Focus Verse: Romans 3:17 (NASB)
"And the path of peace they have not known."

DEVOTION

A woman who had spent years seeking fulfillment in relationships, career success, and material possessions shared her story of constantly feeling restless and dissatisfied. "No matter what I achieved or who I was with, there was always this deep emptiness inside. I didn't understand why I couldn't find peace." It wasn't until she encountered the gospel that she finally experienced the peace she had been searching for. "Jesus gave me the peace I had been chasing for so long," she said.

Paul describes the sinful state of humanity as one that doesn't know the "path of peace." Sin disrupts not only our relationship with God but also our inner peace and our relationships with others. The world offers many paths that promise peace, whether through success, wealth, or pleasure—but none of them lead to true peace. The only path to real, lasting peace is found in Christ.

Sin leads to conflict, anxiety, and unrest. It creates division between us and God, and it fosters discontentment within our hearts. The path of peace that God offers through Jesus is one that restores our relationship with Him, calms our inner turmoil, and leads us into harmony with others. It is a peace that surpasses understanding, rooted in the assurance of God's love and grace.

As believers, we are called to walk the path of peace, both in our relationship with God and in how we interact with others. Let's seek to be peacemakers, living out the peace we have received from Christ and sharing it with those around us.

FURTHER READING
Isaiah 26:3; John 14:27; Philippians 4:6-7

PRAYER
Lord, thank You for the peace You offer through Christ. Help me to walk in that peace every day, trusting in Your love and sharing Your peace with others. Amen.

CHALLENGE
Think about the areas of your life where you may be seeking peace in things other than God. Surrender those areas to Him, and ask for His peace to fill your heart and guide your steps.

DAY 4: ACCOUNTABILITY TO GOD

Scripture Reading: Romans 3:19-20
Focus Verse: Romans 3:19 (NASB)

"Now we know that whatever the Law says, it speaks to
those who are under the Law, so that every mouth may be
closed and all the world may become accountable to God."

DEVOTION

A young professional had lived much of his life with the mindset
that as long as he followed society's rules and avoided major mistakes, he
was fine. However, after hearing a sermon on God's perfect standard, he
realized that he had been measuring himself by human standards rather
than God's. "I had always assumed that if I was a good person by the
world's standards, I didn't have to worry about anything. But when I
heard that we're all accountable to God's perfect law, I understood how
much I needed grace."

Paul's message in Romans 3:19-20 is sobering: all the world is accountable to God. The Law reveals our sin and leaves us without excuse.
No matter how much we try to justify ourselves or point to our good
deeds, we all fall short of God's perfect standard. The Law silences our
excuses and leaves us in need of a Savior. It reminds us that we cannot
earn our righteousness or stand before God based on our own merits.

As believers, this truth should humble us. We are not saved because
of anything we have done but solely because of God's grace through Jesus Christ. We live in a world that tries to minimize sin or excuse it by
comparing ourselves to others, but before God's Law, all are guilty. This
should stir in us a deep gratitude for the gift of salvation and a desire to
share the message of grace with those who are still trying to justify themselves through their own efforts.

FURTHER READING
Galatians 3:22-24; James 2:10; 1 John 1:8

PRAYER
Father, thank You for revealing my need for Your grace. Help me to live in humility, knowing that I am accountable to You and that it is only through Jesus that I am made righteous. Amen.

CHALLENGE
This week, reflect on how God's Law reveals areas in your life where you fall short. Thank Him for the grace that covers those areas, and commit to living in a way that reflects gratitude for His mercy.

DAY 5: JUSTIFIED BY FAITH

Scripture Reading: Romans 3:21-24
Focus Verse: Romans 3:22 (NASB)
"Even the righteousness of God through faith in Jesus Christ
for all those who believe; for there is no distinction."

DEVOTION

A man who had grown up in a religious family spent years trying to "earn" God's approval through good works. He served in the church, helped others, and tried his best to live a moral life. But despite all his efforts, he never felt truly at peace with God. It wasn't until he heard a message on being justified by faith that his perspective changed. "I realized that I had been trying to earn what God was offering me freely through Jesus," he shared. "It was like a weight had been lifted off my shoulders."

Paul introduces a transformative truth in Romans 3:21-24: we are justified by faith, not by works. This righteousness from God is available to all who believe in Jesus Christ, and it is offered without distinction. Whether Jew or Gentile, religious or non-religious, the same faith that justifies one person justifies all. It is a gift that cannot be earned but is freely given through the grace of God.

This truth should bring immense freedom and joy to our hearts. No longer do we have to strive to earn God's approval; instead, we can rest in the finished work of Jesus. Justification by faith means that our standing before God is secure, not because of what we have done but because of what Christ has done on our behalf. This is the heart of the gospel, and it should compel us to live in gratitude and trust in God's grace.

FURTHER READING

Ephesians 2:8-9; Galatians 2:16; Philippians 3:9

PRAYER

Lord, thank You for justifying me by faith and not by works. Help me to rest in Your grace and to live in the freedom that comes from trusting in Jesus. Amen.

CHALLENGE

Reflect on areas of your life where you may still be striving for God's approval through works. Surrender those areas to Him and embrace the truth that you are justified by faith alone.

DAY 6: REDEMPTION IN CHRIST

Scripture Reading: Romans 3:25-26
Focus Verse: Romans 3:25 (NASB)
"Whom God displayed publicly as a propi-
tiation in His blood through faith."

DEVOTION

A woman who had experienced years of guilt over past mistakes shared how she struggled to believe that God could forgive her. "I felt like I had done too much wrong to be redeemed," she said. But one day, while reading Romans 3:25, she finally understood the depth of Christ's sacrifice. "Jesus didn't just cover my sins, He paid for them fully. His blood was the price of my redemption. I realized that I was free because of what He had done, not because of what I could do."

Paul explains that Jesus' sacrifice was a "propitiation," a payment that satisfied the righteous wrath of God. Through His blood, Christ redeemed us, paying the full price for our sin. This act of redemption wasn't done in secret but was displayed publicly for all to see. Jesus' death on the cross is the ultimate demonstration of God's love and justice.

As believers, we need to grasp the weight of what Christ has done for us. His sacrifice wasn't just a symbolic act, it was the full payment for every sin we've ever committed. This understanding should lead us to live in awe of His love and in gratitude for the freedom we now have. Our redemption is complete, and we no longer live under the weight of guilt and shame. We are free because of Jesus.

FURTHER READING

Colossians 1:13-14; 1 John 2:2; Hebrews 9:12

PRAYER

Jesus, thank You for redeeming me through Your blood. Help me to live in the freedom You have purchased for me, and may my life reflect the gratitude I feel for Your sacrifice. Amen.

CHALLENGE

This week, meditate on the fact that Jesus' blood paid the full price for your redemption. Let go of any lingering guilt or shame and embrace the freedom you have in Christ.

DAY 7: BOASTING EXCLUDED

Scripture Reading: Romans 3:27-31
Focus Verse: Romans 3:27 (NASB)
"Where then is boasting? It is excluded. By what kind
of law? Of works? No, but by a law of faith."

DEVOTION

A competitive athlete was used to boasting about his achievements, both on and off the field. He had always prided himself on his hard work and determination. However, when he came to faith, he realized that in God's Kingdom, there was no place for boasting. "Everything I have is a gift from God," he said. "Even my faith is not something I earned; it's something He gave me. There's nothing for me to boast about except in what Christ has done."

Paul makes it clear that in the gospel, boasting is excluded. We are not saved by our works or efforts, but by faith in what Christ has done. This leaves no room for pride or self-congratulation. The law of faith humbles us, reminding us that salvation is entirely a gift from God.

This truth frees us from the need to compare ourselves to others or to try to "outdo" anyone in righteousness. In God's eyes, we are all equally in need of grace, and it is His work, not ours, that saves us. Let's remember that every good thing in our lives is a result of God's grace, and let's boast only in the Lord.

FURTHER READING

1 Corinthians 1:28-31; Ephesians 2:8-9; Jeremiah 9:23-24

PRAYER

Father, thank You for reminding me that there is no room for boasting in my salvation. Help me to always point to You as the source of every blessing and to boast only in what Christ has done for me. Amen.

CHALLENGE

This week, take time to reflect on areas where you may be tempted to boast or take credit for what God has done. Redirect your praise to Him and remember that all glory belongs to the Lord.

WALKING FURTHER:
WEEK 5 QUESTIONS

1. How does Paul's statement that "none is righteous" challenge the way we view ourselves and others? How does this truth deepen your appreciation for grace?

2. Why does Paul describe sinful speech as "poison"? In what ways can our words build up or destroy? How can you be more intentional about using your words to reflect Christ?

3. What does it mean to walk the "path of peace" in a world full of conflict and unrest? How can you seek and promote peace in your relationships and circumstances?

4. Paul speaks about the Law silencing every excuse and leaving the world accountable to God. How does this impact your understanding of accountability? How can we live with this awareness in our daily lives?

5. Justification by faith is central to the gospel. How does this truth bring you freedom from striving and a deeper reliance on God's grace?

6. In what ways does understanding redemption through Christ's blood change the way you view your identity and worth? How can this truth free you from guilt or shame?

7. Why does the gospel exclude boasting? How can you cultivate a heart of humility that points to Christ as the source of all that you have and all that you are?

WEEK 6: JUSTIFICATION BY FAITH
(ROMANS 4)

FAITH CREDITED AS RIGHTEOUSNESS
- ROMANS 4:1-3

GOD WHO JUSTIFIES THE UNGODLY
- ROMANS 4:4-5

DAVID'S JOY IN FORGIVENESS
- ROMANS 4:6-8

RIGHTEOUSNESS APART FROM CIRCUMCISION
- ROMANS 4:9-12

HEIR OF THE WORLD BY FAITH
- ROMANS 4:13-15

FAITH IN THE FACE OF THE IMPOSSIBLE
- ROMANS 4:16-18

FAITH IN GOD'S POWER
- ROMANS 4:19-25

DAY 1: FAITH CREDITED AS RIGHTEOUSNESS

Scripture Reading: Romans 4:1-3
Focus Verse: Romans 4:3 (NASB)
"For what does the Scripture say? 'Abraham believed
God, and it was credited to him as righteousness.'"

DEVOTION

A farmer, who spent his whole life working tirelessly, once shared his journey of faith. For years, he thought that his hard work, both in life and faith, would earn him a place with God. He tried to "do enough good" to balance out his failures, but it left him weary and frustrated. It wasn't until a pastor explained to him that righteousness comes through faith, not works, that the truth finally set him free. "It was like a weight lifted off my shoulders. I realized God wanted my trust, not my perfect performance."

Paul draws on the story of Abraham to emphasize a foundational truth: righteousness is credited through faith, not by works. Abraham wasn't considered righteous because of his actions, but because he believed God. This is the heart of the gospel: our standing before God is not based on our efforts but on our faith in His promises.

This truth is liberating. Like the farmer, many of us spend too much time trying to earn God's favor, thinking that if we do enough good, God will accept us. But Scripture makes it clear: faith, not works, is what God credits as righteousness. This doesn't mean that our actions don't matter, but rather that they flow from a heart of faith, not as a means to earn salvation.

Let this reminder bring you peace today. God's desire is for you to trust Him fully, just as Abraham did. When we believe in God's promises, He credits us with righteousness, not because of what we've done, but because of what Christ has done.

FURTHER READING

Genesis 15:6; Galatians 3:6-9; James 2:23

PRAYER

Lord, thank You for crediting me with righteousness through faith, just as You did for Abraham. Help me to trust in Your promises and rest in the work that Christ has done on my behalf. Amen.

CHALLENGE

Consider areas of your life where you might still be striving for God's approval through your own efforts. Surrender those areas to Him and embrace the truth that righteousness comes through faith, not works.

DAY 2: GOD WHO JUSTIFIES THE UNGODLY

Scripture Reading: Romans 4:4-5
Focus Verse: Romans 4:5 (NASB)
"But to the one who does not work, but believes in Him who justifies the ungodly, his faith is credited as righteousness."

DEVOTION

A young man, who lived a life far from God, had made countless mistakes. After years of running from God, he hit rock bottom and thought he was beyond redemption. One day, a friend shared Romans 4:5 with him, explaining that God justifies the ungodly. "It was like a lightbulb moment," the man recalled. "I didn't have to clean myself up before coming to God. He was ready to justify me, just as I was, if I would believe in Him."

The message of grace is radical. God justifies the ungodly. Not the righteous, not those who seem to have their lives together, but those who are broken and lost. This is the power of the gospel: God takes those who are far from Him, and through faith, He declares them righteous. Paul emphasizes that it is not through works, but through faith, that this justification occurs.

For many, this truth is difficult to accept because we're conditioned to believe that we must work to earn approval. But God's way is different. He offers justification freely to those who believe, even if they've lived a life far from Him. This should fill us with awe and gratitude, knowing that God's grace is greater than our failures.

If you've ever felt unworthy of God's love, remember that He justifies the ungodly through faith. There is nothing you need to do to earn it. Simply believe in Him, and your faith will be credited as righteousness.

FURTHER READING

Titus 3:5-7; Ephesians 2:8-9; Luke 18:9-14

PRAYER

Father, thank You for justifying me through faith, even when I was far from You. Help me to remember that Your grace is not earned but freely given. I trust in Your promises and rest in Your righteousness. Amen.

CHALLENGE

Take a moment to reflect on the incredible grace of God, who justifies the ungodly. Share this message of grace with someone who might feel unworthy of God's love.

DAY 3: DAVID'S JOY IN FORGIVENESS

Scripture Reading: Romans 4:6-8
Focus Verse: Romans 4:7 (NASB)
"'Blessed are those whose lawless deeds have been forgiven, and whose sins have been covered.'"

DEVOTION

A woman who had carried the weight of past mistakes for years finally found peace after reading Psalm 32, the passage Paul references in Romans 4:6-8. "I had always believed that my past sins defined me," she said. "But when I read David's words about forgiveness and how God covers our sins, I realized that God had forgiven me and that I didn't need to carry the guilt any longer."

David's joy in forgiveness, as quoted by Paul, is a reminder of the profound blessing of having our sins forgiven. David knew the weight of guilt and shame but also the joy of being forgiven by God. Forgiveness is not something we can earn; it is a gift from God through His grace. When our sins are forgiven and covered, we are freed from the burden of guilt and able to live in the joy of God's love.

This forgiveness is not just about God wiping our slate clean, it's about Him covering our sins, meaning they are no longer visible in His sight. In Christ, we are made new, and our sins are not held against us. Just as David rejoiced in the blessing of forgiveness, we too can experience that same joy, knowing that our sins have been fully covered by the blood of Jesus.

If you're struggling with guilt or shame from your past, remember that God has forgiven you. Your sins are covered, and you are free to walk in His grace and joy.

FURTHER READING
Psalm 32:1-2; Isaiah 43:25; 1 John 1:9

PRAYER
Lord, thank You for the joy of forgiveness. Help me to live in the freedom that comes from knowing my sins are covered by Your grace. I praise You for Your mercy and love. Amen.

CHALLENGE
Think about any areas in your life where you may still be holding onto guilt or shame. Bring those areas before God and allow Him to cover your sins with His forgiveness.

DAY 4: RIGHTEOUSNESS APART FROM CIRCUMCISION

Scripture Reading: Romans 4:9-12
Focus Verse: Romans 4:10 (NASB)
"How then was it credited? While he was circumcised, or un-circumcised? Not while circumcised, but while uncircumcised."

DEVOTION

A young believer, who had recently come to faith, shared how she often felt inadequate because she hadn't grown up in a Christian home or followed certain religious traditions. "I thought that because I didn't have the same background as others, maybe my faith wasn't enough," she said. "But then I learned that it's not about rituals or traditions, it's about faith, just like with Abraham."

Paul's point in Romans 4:9-12 is that Abraham was credited with righteousness before he was circumcised. This means that righteousness comes through faith, not through rituals or religious practices. Circumcision, for the Jews, was a sign of the covenant, but Paul makes it clear that Abraham's righteousness came before any outward sign.

This is an important truth for all believers. It reminds us that our standing with God is based on faith, not on religious rituals or practices. While outward expressions of faith are important, they do not save us. We are made righteous by our faith in God, just as Abraham was. This truth levels the playing field whether we come from a long line of believers or are new to the faith, righteousness is credited by faith alone.

Let's embrace this truth and live with the confidence that our righteousness comes from God's grace, not from our background, traditions, or outward actions.

FURTHER READING

Galatians 5:6; Colossians 2:11-14; Philippians 3:3

PRAYER

Father, thank You for the reminder that righteousness comes through faith, not through rituals or traditions. Help me to live in the freedom of Your grace and to trust fully in You. Amen.

CHALLENGE

Consider whether there are any religious practices or traditions that you've relied on for your sense of righteousness. Surrender those to God and remember that faith alone is what makes you righteous before Him.

DAY 5: HEIR OF THE WORLD BY FAITH

Scripture Reading: Romans 4:13-15
Focus Verse: Romans 4:13 (NASB)
"For the promise to Abraham or to his descendants
that he would be heir of the world was not through
the Law, but through the righteousness of faith."

DEVOTION

A man who had spent most of his life trying to "earn" his place in his family's business shared how exhausting it was to feel like everything depended on his performance. He lived in constant fear of failure, believing that his inheritance would be taken away if he didn't measure up. "When I became a Christian," he said, "I learned that God's promises don't work like that. They're not something I earn, they're a gift through faith. I realized I didn't have to live in fear anymore."

Paul's words in Romans 4:13 remind us that God's promises are received through faith, not through works or the Law. Abraham's inheritance—the promise that he would be heir of the world—was not given because he kept the Law (the Law hadn't even been given yet). Instead, the promise was based on Abraham's faith. This principle still holds true for us today. As heirs of God's Kingdom, we receive His promises by faith, not by our performance or adherence to the Law.

This truth sets us free from the fear of failure or the burden of trying to "earn" God's favor. Just as Abraham trusted God's promises and was declared righteous, we too are called to live by faith. Our inheritance in Christ is secure, not because of what we've done, but because of what God has promised. Let's walk in the confidence that we are heirs of God's promises by faith and not by works.

FURTHER READING

Galatians 3:18; Hebrews 6:13-15; Ephesians 2:8-9

PRAYER

Lord, thank You that Your promises are received through faith and not by works. Help me to trust in Your Word and to walk confidently in the inheritance I have through Christ. Amen.

CHALLENGE

Reflect on any areas of your life where you've been trying to "earn" God's favor. Release those areas to Him, and rest in the knowledge that His promises are received by faith alone.

DAY 6: FAITH IN THE FACE OF THE IMPOSSIBLE

Scripture Reading: Romans 4:16-18
Focus Verse: Romans 4:18 (NASB)
"In hope against hope he believed, so that he might become a father of many nations according to that which had been spoken, 'So shall your descendants be.'"

DEVOTION

A couple who had struggled with infertility for years were told by doctors that they would never have children. Despite the odds, they continued to pray and trust God, believing that He was able to do the impossible. Several years later, they welcomed a baby boy into their family. "We held on to God's promises, even when everything around us said it was impossible," they shared. "We learned what it means to have faith in the face of the impossible."

Abraham's story is one of extraordinary faith. Despite being old and childless, he believed God's promise that he would become the father of many nations. Paul highlights that Abraham had faith "in hope against hope," meaning that he believed even when circumstances seemed impossible. His faith wasn't based on what he could see, but on the faithfulness of the God who had made the promise.

As believers, we are called to have that same kind of faith, a faith that trusts God's promises, even when circumstances seem hopeless. Whether it's waiting for a breakthrough in a difficult situation or trusting God's word when everything around us seems to contradict it, we are invited to believe in God's faithfulness. Abraham's story reminds us that God is not limited by what seems impossible. His promises stand firm, and He is always able to fulfill them.

FURTHER READING

Genesis 17:1-5; Hebrews 11:11-12; Mark 9:23

PRAYER

Father, help me to have faith like Abraham, to believe Your promises even in the face of impossible circumstances. Strengthen my trust in Your faithfulness, knowing that nothing is too difficult for You. Amen.

CHALLENGE

Is there a situation in your life that seems impossible? Surrender it to God today and ask Him to strengthen your faith as you trust in His promises, even when the outcome seems uncertain.

DAY 7: FAITH IN GOD'S POWER

Scripture Reading: Romans 4:19-25
Focus Verse: Romans 4:21 (NASB)
"And being fully assured that what God had promised, He was able also to perform."

DEVOTION

A woman who had been diagnosed with a serious illness shared how her faith carried her through a long season of uncertainty. "There were days when I didn't know if I would make it through, but I held on to one thing: God is able. I trusted that no matter what happened, He had the power to carry me through, whether by healing or by giving me strength to endure."

Abraham's faith was rooted in his confidence in God's power. He believed that if God had made a promise, He was fully able to fulfill it, regardless of the circumstances. This kind of faith doesn't come from wishful thinking or blind optimism, it comes from knowing who God is and trusting in His character and ability. Abraham's unwavering trust in God's power is what allowed him to hope in the face of impossibility.

For us, faith in God's power is essential. We may face challenges that seem insurmountable, but we serve a God who is able to do exceedingly and abundantly beyond all we can ask or think (Ephesians 3:20). Our faith is not in our ability to figure things out, but in God's ability to fulfill His promises. When we trust in God's power, we can face any situation with confidence, knowing that He is always able to perform what He has promised.

FURTHER READING

Luke 1:37; Jeremiah 32:17; Romans 8:31

PRAYER

Lord, thank You for Your great power and faithfulness. Help me to trust fully in Your ability to fulfill every promise You've made. Strengthen my faith, and give me confidence in Your power, no matter what challenges I face. Amen.

CHALLENGE

Think about a promise of God that you are waiting to see fulfilled. Commit to trusting in His power, not in your circumstances, and ask Him to strengthen your faith as you wait on His timing.

WALKING FURTHER:
WEEK 6 QUESTIONS

1. What does it mean for righteousness to be credited through faith, as it was for Abraham? How does this truth impact your view of salvation and grace?

2. How does the concept of God justifying the ungodly challenge the way you view grace and forgiveness? In what ways can you extend that same grace to others?

3. David speaks of the blessing of forgiveness. How can you cultivate a deeper sense of gratitude for the forgiveness you've received in Christ?

4. Why is it important to understand that righteousness comes apart from religious rituals or traditions? How does this free us to live in relationship with God rather than legalism?

5. How does knowing that you are an heir of God's promises by faith (and not by works) change the way you live? In what ways can you embrace the freedom that comes from being a child of God?

6. When have you experienced "faith in the face of the impossible"? How can Abraham's example of faith inspire you in situations where the outcome seems uncertain?

7. What does it mean to be "fully assured" of God's power, as Abraham was? How can you grow in confidence in God's ability to fulfill His promises in your life?

WEEK 7: PEACE WITH GOD THROUGH CHRIST (ROMANS 5)

PEACE WITH GOD
- ROMANS 5:1

REJOICING IN SUFFERING
- ROMANS 5:2-3

GOD'S LOVE POURED OUT
- ROMANS 5:5

CHRIST DIED FOR US
- ROMANS 5:6-8

SAVED FROM WRATH
- ROMANS 5:9-10

RECONCILIATION THROUGH CHRIST
- ROMANS 5:11

LIFE THROUGH CHRIST
- ROMANS 5:12-21

DAY 1: PEACE WITH GOD

Scripture Reading: Romans 5:1
Focus Verse: Romans 5:1 (NASB)
"Therefore, having been justified by faith, we have
peace with God through our Lord Jesus Christ."

DEVOTION

David, a man who had struggled with anxiety and a sense of guilt
for years, always felt like something was off in his relationship with God.
Despite his efforts to do the right thing, he never felt fully at peace.
During a retreat, a speaker shared this verse from Romans 5:1, explaining
that peace with God is not something we earn through our behavior, it's
something we receive through faith in Jesus Christ. David said, "For the
first time, I realized that my peace with God didn't depend on how good
I was, but on what Jesus had already done for me."

Paul's declaration that we have peace with God through our Lord
Jesus Christ is one of the most profound truths of the gospel. Before we
come to faith in Christ, we are estranged from God, separated from Him
because of our sin. But when we are justified by faith—declared righteous
in God's sight because of Jesus' sacrifice—our relationship with God is
restored, and we can experience true peace.

This peace is more than just a feeling of calm. It's a deep, abiding
sense of reconciliation with God. No longer are we His enemies; we are
now His children, fully accepted and loved. This peace with God is the
foundation of our relationship with Him. It frees us from guilt, shame,
and the fear of punishment because we know that Jesus has paid the price
for our sins.

If you've been striving for peace with God through your own efforts,
rest in the truth that peace is a gift that comes through faith in Christ.
Embrace the peace that Jesus offers, knowing that you are fully reconciled
to God.

FURTHER READING

Ephesians 2:14-16; Colossians 1:20-22; Philippians 4:7

PRAYER

Lord, thank You for the peace I have with You through Jesus Christ. Help me to rest in the assurance of Your love and to live in the freedom that comes from knowing I am reconciled to You. Amen.

CHALLENGE

Reflect on what it means to have peace with God. Are there areas where you're still trying to earn His approval? Let go of those efforts and embrace the peace that comes through faith in Christ.

DAY 2: REJOICING IN SUFFERING

Scripture Reading: Romans 5:2-3
Focus Verse: Romans 5:3 (NASB)
"And not only this, but we also exult in our tribulations,
knowing that tribulation brings about perseverance."

DEVOTION

Sarah had always believed that if she followed God, her life would be free from major struggles. So when she faced a series of personal trials, including losing her job and a family health crisis, she was devastated. It wasn't until she studied Romans 5:2-3 that she began to see her suffering in a new light. "I realized that God wasn't punishing me," Sarah said. "He was using these trials to strengthen my faith. I learned to rejoice in the midst of suffering because I saw how God was shaping me through it."

Rejoicing in suffering is a countercultural concept, but Paul teaches us that suffering has a purpose in the life of a believer. Instead of leading to despair, trials produce perseverance, which in turn builds character and strengthens our hope in God. When we face difficulties, it's natural to want to avoid them, but Paul reminds us that God uses these moments to refine us.

Rejoicing in suffering doesn't mean we enjoy pain or hardship, but it does mean that we can have a deep sense of joy, knowing that God is working in and through our circumstances. He uses trials to grow our faith, deepen our dependence on Him, and prepare us for the future He has planned for us. When we understand that God is with us in our suffering, we can endure it with hope, knowing that He will use it for our good.

If you are facing challenges today, remember that God is at work, even in your suffering. Trust that He is producing perseverance in you and that your trials are not in vain.

FURTHER READING

James 1:2-4; 2 Corinthians 4:17-18; 1 Peter 1:6-7

PRAYER

Father, help me to trust You in the midst of my trials. Give me the strength to rejoice, knowing that You are producing perseverance and character in me through every hardship. Amen.

CHALLENGE

Think about a current or past trial you've faced. How can you begin to see God's hand in that situation? Spend time in prayer, asking Him to show you how He is using your suffering for His purposes.

DAY 3: GOD'S LOVE POURED OUT

Scripture Reading: Romans 5:5
Focus Verse: Romans 5:5 (NASB)
"And hope does not disappoint, because the love
of God has been poured out within our hearts
through the Holy Spirit who was given to us."

DEVOTION

Tom, a man who had grown up feeling unloved and unwanted, spent years searching for acceptance. No matter what he achieved, the emptiness remained. One day, a friend invited him to church, where he heard a sermon on Romans 5:5. "For the first time, I realized that God's love wasn't something I had to earn, it was something He poured into me," Tom shared. "Knowing that His love was already mine, through the Holy Spirit, changed everything. I no longer had to chase approval."

The love of God is not something we strive to achieve; it is something He freely pours out into our hearts through the Holy Spirit. This love is a gift that reassures us, fills us with hope, and sustains us through life's trials. When we face difficulties, it's easy to feel alone or abandoned, but Paul reminds us that God's love has already been poured into us. The Holy Spirit is the evidence of that love, dwelling within us and reminding us daily of God's care and commitment to us.

God's love is not conditional or based on our performance. It is a love that endures, no matter what we face. The presence of the Holy Spirit in our lives is the constant reminder of that love. He is the one who fills our hearts with the assurance that we belong to God and are deeply loved by Him.

If you're feeling discouraged or unloved today, take heart. God's love is already poured out within you through the Holy Spirit. Trust in the unfailing love of your heavenly Father, knowing that His love never fails, and it never runs dry.

FURTHER READING
Ephesians 3:17-19; 1 John 4:16-18; Titus 3:5-6

PRAYER
Lord, thank You for pouring out Your love into my heart through the Holy Spirit. Help me to live in the fullness of that love and to remember that I am never alone, for Your love is always with me. Amen.

CHALLENGE
Spend time in prayer this week, asking the Holy Spirit to help you experience the depth of God's love. Let that love shape the way you respond to others, knowing that you are loved unconditionally by your heavenly Father.

DAY 4: CHRIST DIED FOR US

Scripture Reading: Romans 5:6-8
Focus Verse: Romans 5:8 (NASB)
"But God demonstrates His own love toward us, in
that while we were yet sinners, Christ died for us."

DEVOTION

John grew up believing that in order to be accepted by God, he had to clean up his life first. He thought he had to be "good enough" before God would love him. One evening, while reading Romans 5:8, the truth finally hit him. "It said, 'While we were yet sinners, Christ died for us.' That means He loved me even at my worst," John said. "I didn't have to fix myself before coming to Him. Christ loved me and died for me right where I was."

Romans 5:8 reveals the heart of the gospel: while we were still sinners, Christ died for us. God didn't wait for us to clean ourselves up or get our act together before demonstrating His love. He loved us at our worst, and in that love, He sent Christ to die for us. This truth shatters the lie that we need to be "good enough" for God. His love is freely given, not because of who we are, but because of who He is.

God's love is not conditional. He doesn't love us more when we are obedient or less when we fail. His love is constant, and it was most clearly displayed at the cross. Jesus died for us while we were still far from God, and through His sacrifice, we are brought near. This is the foundation of our faith: the overwhelming love of God that pursued us even in our sin.

If you've ever felt unworthy of God's love, remember that Christ died for you, not because you were perfect, but because He loves you unconditionally. Rest in that love today, knowing that nothing can separate you from it.

FURTHER READING

Ephesians 2:4-5; John 15:13; 1 John 4:9-10

PRAYER

Father, thank You for loving me even when I was far from You. Thank You for sending Christ to die for me while I was still a sinner. Help me to live in the light of Your love, trusting that nothing can separate me from You. Amen.

CHALLENGE

Take time to reflect on the fact that Christ died for you while you were still a sinner. Let this truth sink deeply into your heart and share it with someone who might need to hear about God's unconditional love.

DAY 5: SAVED FROM WRATH

Scripture Reading: Romans 5:9-10
Focus Verse: Romans 5:9 (NASB)
"Much more then, having now been justified by His blood,
we shall be saved from the wrath of God through Him."

DEVOTION

Michael had always been anxious about God's judgment. He feared that no matter what he did, he would never be good enough to escape God's wrath. But when his pastor explained Romans 5:9, everything changed. "I realized that Jesus took the wrath I deserved," Michael shared. "I didn't need to live in fear anymore because Christ's blood covered me and saved me from judgment. The weight of that fear was lifted."

The truth of Romans 5:9 is both humbling and comforting: because of Christ's sacrifice, we are saved from the wrath of God. As sinners, we were all deserving of God's righteous judgment, but through Jesus' death, we are justified—declared righteous by His blood. Instead of facing wrath, we receive grace. This is the essence of the gospel: Christ stood in our place, took the punishment we deserved, and made a way for us to be reconciled to God.

This reality should bring us peace. As believers, we no longer need to fear God's wrath because Jesus bore it for us on the cross. We are now clothed in His righteousness, and our future is secure. The wrath of God that once hung over us has been removed, and in its place, we have peace with God and the promise of eternal life.

If you've been living in fear of God's judgment, remember that Christ has already paid the price. You are saved from wrath through Him, and nothing can change that. Rest in the assurance of your salvation, knowing that you are safe in God's hands.

FURTHER READING

1 Thessalonians 5:9; Ephesians 2:3-5; John 3:36

PRAYER

Lord, thank You for saving me from Your wrath through Jesus' sacrifice. Help me to live in the peace that comes from knowing I am justified by His blood and safe in Your love. Amen.

CHALLENGE

Reflect on the truth that Christ has saved you from God's wrath. If you've been living in fear or anxiety about your salvation, bring those fears to God in prayer and thank Him for the security you have in Christ.

DAY 6: RECONCILIATION THROUGH CHRIST

Scripture Reading: Romans 5:11
Focus Verse: Romans 5:11 (NASB)
"And not only this, but we also exult in God
through our Lord Jesus Christ, through whom
we have now received the reconciliation."

DEVOTION

Julie always felt like something was missing in her relationship with God. Even though she attended church and read the Bible, she never felt fully connected. One day, while studying Romans 5:11, she realized that through Jesus, she had already been reconciled to God. "I wasn't striving for reconciliation anymore," Julie said. "It had already been given to me through Christ. I finally understood that I was fully accepted and at peace with God."

Reconciliation is the restoration of a broken relationship, and through Christ, we have been reconciled to God. Our sin once separated us from Him, but through Jesus' death and resurrection, that barrier has been removed. Now, we are no longer enemies of God. We are His children, fully accepted and loved. This reconciliation is not something we earn; it's a gift that we receive by faith.

Paul calls us to "exult" in this reconciliation, to rejoice in the fact that our relationship with God has been restored. No longer do we have to strive for acceptance or live under the weight of our sin. In Christ, we are fully reconciled to God, and that is something to celebrate. We can live in the joy of knowing that we are at peace with our Creator, not because of what we've done, but because of what Christ has done for us.

If you've been feeling distant from God, remember that reconciliation is already yours through Jesus. You don't have to work for it, it's a gift. Embrace the truth that you are fully accepted by God, and let that reality fill you with joy and peace.

FURTHER READING
2 Corinthians 5:18-19; Colossians 1:20-22; Ephesians 2:13-16

PRAYER
Father, thank You for reconciling me to Yourself through Jesus Christ. Help me to live in the joy of that reconciliation, knowing that I am fully accepted and loved by You. Amen.

CHALLENGE
Take time to reflect on your reconciliation with God through Christ. How does this truth impact the way you live? Spend time thanking God for restoring your relationship with Him, and share this good news with someone who needs to hear it.

DAY 7: LIFE THROUGH CHRIST

Scripture Reading: Romans 5:12-21
Focus Verse: Romans 5:17 (NASB)
"For if by the transgression of the one, death reigned
through the one, much more those who receive the
abundance of grace and of the gift of righteousness
will reign in life through the One, Jesus Christ."

DEVOTION

David always struggled with guilt and shame from his past. He believed his mistakes defined him and that he could never truly be free from them. One day, while reading Romans 5, David realized that his past didn't have to determine his future. Just as sin came into the world through Adam and brought death, grace and righteousness come through Jesus Christ, bringing new life. This truth changed David's life. He began to live in the freedom that comes from knowing he was no longer condemned by his past but made alive in Christ.

In Romans 5:12-21, Paul contrasts the effects of Adam's sin with the life-giving work of Christ. Through Adam's disobedience, sin and death entered the world, affecting all humanity. But through Jesus' obedience, righteousness and life are made available to everyone who believes. Where Adam's failure brought death, Jesus' sacrifice brings abundant grace and eternal life.

This passage reminds us of the victory we have in Christ. The power of sin and death no longer has a hold on those who are in Jesus. Just as David learned, our past no longer defines us. Instead, we can reign in life through the abundance of grace that comes from Christ. Are you living in the fullness of this grace, or are you allowing the weight of your past to hinder you from experiencing the life Jesus offers?

FURTHER READING

1 Corinthians 15:21-22; John 10:10; Ephesians 2:4-6

PRAYER

Father, thank You for the new life You have given us through Jesus Christ. Help me to walk in the fullness of Your grace, leaving behind the weight of sin and shame. May I live each day in the joy of knowing that I am free and alive in Christ. Amen.

CHALLENGE

Take a moment to reflect on how the grace of Christ has transformed your life. Is there an area where you are still allowing your past to define you? Surrender that to God and walk in the freedom of His grace. Share this message of life through Christ with someone who needs encouragement today.

WALKING FURTHER:
WEEK 7

1. Reflect on Romans 5:1. How has your understanding of peace with God deepened through this week's devotions? How does this peace influence your daily life?

2. In Romans 5:3-4, Paul teaches that suffering produces perseverance, character, and hope. Can you recall a time when suffering led to growth in your faith?

3. How does knowing that "Christ died for us while we were still sinners" (Romans 5:8) impact your view of God's love?

4. Romans 5:10-11 talks about being reconciled to God through the death of His Son. How has this reconciliation, through Christ death, changed your relationship with God?

5. How does Romans 5:12-21 describe the impact of Adam's sin and Christ's righteousness?

6. In Romans 5:17, Paul talks about receiving the "abundance of grace" and reigning in life through Christ. What does living in this grace look like in practical terms for you? How can you reign over the struggles or sins that try to hold you back?

7. What role does the Holy Spirit play in pouring God's love into our hearts (Romans 5:5)? Reflect on the work of the Holy Spirit in your life. How can you become more aware of His presence and allow Him to fill you with God's love?

WEEK 8:
NEW LIFE IN CHRIST
(ROMANS 6)

DEAD TO SIN, ALIVE IN CHRIST
  – ROMANS 6:1-2

BAPTIZED INTO HIS DEATH
  – ROMANS 6:3-4

UNITED WITH CHRIST
  – ROMANS 6:5-7

CONSIDER YOURSELF DEAD TO SIN
  – ROMANS 6:8-11

PRESENT YOURSELF TO GOD
  – ROMANS 6:12-14

SLAVES OF RIGHTEOUSNESS
  – ROMANS 6:15-18

THE WAGES OF SIN IS DEATH
  – ROMANS 6:19-23

DAY 1: DEAD TO SIN, ALIVE IN CHRIST

Scripture Reading: Romans 6:1-2
Focus Verse: Romans 6:2 (NASB)
"May it never be! How shall we who died to sin still live in it?"

DEVOTION

Karen had struggled with the same sin for years, feeling defeated and discouraged. One day, during a Bible study, they read Romans 6:2, and the words hit her with new clarity. "If I am truly dead to sin, why am I letting it control me?" she thought. From that moment, she decided to live in the truth of her new identity, believing that through Christ, she was no longer bound by her old patterns.

Paul's message is revolutionary: if we have died to sin, we are no longer bound to live in it. When we accepted Christ, our old self was crucified with Him, and we were given a new life. This doesn't mean that we'll never struggle with sin, but it does mean that sin no longer has power over us. We are now alive in Christ, empowered by His Spirit to live a life that pleases God.

Being "dead to sin" means that we no longer live under its influence or control. Our identity has changed. We are new creations in Christ. The enemy may try to convince us otherwise, but we must stand firm in this truth. Each day, we have a choice to live in the freedom Christ has given us or to fall back into old patterns. When we choose to live in the reality of being alive in Christ, we experience the fullness of the new life He offers.

FURTHER READING

2 Corinthians 5:17; Galatians 2:20; Colossians 3:3

PRAYER

Lord, thank You for setting me free from the power of sin. Help me to live each day as one who is alive in Christ, refusing to let sin control my life. Strengthen me by Your Spirit to walk in newness of life. Amen.

CHALLENGE

Identify an area where you feel trapped in old patterns or habits. Ask God to help you break free, reminding yourself that you are dead to sin and alive in Christ.

DAY 2: BAPTIZED INTO HIS DEATH

Scripture Reading: Romans 6:3-4
Focus Verse: Romans 6:4 (NASB)
"Therefore we have been buried with Him through
baptism into death, so that as Christ was raised
from the dead through the glory of the Father,
so we too might walk in newness of life."

DEVOTION

Mark had been baptized as a young adult, but it wasn't until years later that he fully understood its significance. "I thought baptism was just a symbol," he shared. "But then I realized it represented my own death and resurrection with Christ. Baptism wasn't just about getting wet, it was about entering a new life." This deeper understanding transformed how Mark viewed his identity in Christ.

In baptism, we are united with Christ in His death and resurrection. It's not simply a ritual but a powerful declaration that our old life is gone, and we are now alive in Christ. When we go under the water, it symbolizes our burial with Christ, and as we rise, it represents our resurrection to new life. This outward act reflects an inward reality: we are dead to sin and raised to live for God.

Baptism reminds us that we are no longer who we once were. Our past sins, failures, and struggles no longer define us. We have been given a new life, empowered by the Holy Spirit to walk in a way that honors God. As we daily remember our baptism, we can embrace the truth that our old self is buried, and we are now alive with Christ, walking in the newness of life He gives.

FURTHER READING

Colossians 2:12; Galatians 3:27; 1 Peter 3:21

PRAYER

Father, thank You for the gift of new life through Christ's death and resurrection. Help me to live in the reality of my baptism, knowing that my old self is gone and I am now alive in Christ. May my life reflect the newness You have given me. Amen.

CHALLENGE

Reflect on your baptism or the moment you decided to follow Christ. What does it mean for you to walk in newness of life today? Ask God to help you live out this truth in practical ways.

DAY 3: UNITED WITH CHRIST

Scripture Reading: Romans 6:5-7
Focus Verse: Romans 6:5 (NASB)
"For if we have become united with Him in
the likeness of His death, certainly we shall also
be in the likeness of His resurrection."

DEVOTION

Jessica often felt overwhelmed by her past, as if her old mistakes still held her captive. But when she read Romans 6:5, she began to see herself differently. "If I'm united with Christ in His death and resurrection, then I'm not the same person anymore," she realized. "I have new life in Him. My past doesn't define me; Jesus does." This shift helped Jessica find freedom from the guilt and shame that had plagued her.

Paul teaches that as believers, we are united with Christ in both His death and resurrection. This unity means that our old self has been crucified with Him, and we are now resurrected to a new life. Just as Jesus was raised to life, we too are given new, resurrected lives, empowered by the Holy Spirit to live differently.

This union with Christ is foundational to our identity. We no longer belong to our past sins or failures; we belong to Christ. We are free from sin's power and are given the strength to live for God. Understanding this truth helps us to break free from the shame of our past, realizing that our lives are now hidden in Christ. When we embrace our union with Him, we find the courage and strength to live victoriously, walking in the resurrection power He provides.

FURTHER READING

Philippians 3:10-11; Galatians 2:20; 2 Corinthians 5:17

PRAYER

Lord Jesus, thank You for uniting me with You in both Your death and resurrection. Help me to live in the freedom that comes from being united with You, no longer bound by my past but empowered by Your Spirit to live a new life. Amen.

CHALLENGE

Reflect on what it means to be united with Christ in His resurrection. In what areas of your life do you need to embrace this freedom? Surrender those areas to God, trusting in His resurrection power to transform you.

DAY 4: CONSIDER YOURSELF DEAD TO SIN

Scripture Reading: Romans 6:8-11
Focus Verse: Romans 6:11 (NASB)
"Even so consider yourselves to be dead to
sin, but alive to God in Christ Jesus."

DEVOTION

Rachel struggled with guilt and frustration every time she made a mistake. She felt as though she would never overcome certain habits. One day, her mentor pointed her to Romans 6:11 and asked, "Do you see yourself as dead to sin or as a slave to it?" Rachel realized she had been viewing herself from the wrong perspective. "I began to see myself as God sees me: alive in Christ, not bound to sin. That truth changed how I approached my struggles."

Paul challenges us to see ourselves from a new perspective: we are dead to sin and alive to God. This isn't just positive thinking, it's a reality based on our union with Christ. When Jesus died, our old sinful self died with Him. When He rose, we rose to new life with Him. To consider ourselves dead to sin means we recognize that sin no longer defines us or has authority over us.

This perspective empowers us to live differently. When we view ourselves as dead to sin, we're less likely to fall back into old patterns. Instead, we can live fully alive to God, embracing the righteousness He has given us. Each day, let's remind ourselves of this truth, choosing to live out our new identity in Christ rather than our old nature.

FURTHER READING

2 Corinthians 5:17; Colossians 3:3; Galatians 5:24

PRAYER

Lord, thank You for giving me new life in Christ. Help me to see myself as You see me: dead to sin and alive to You. Strengthen me to live in this truth each day. Amen.

CHALLENGE

This week, whenever you face temptation, remind yourself that you are dead to sin and alive to God. Let this truth guide your response and encourage you to walk in victory.

DAY 5: PRESENT YOURSELF TO GOD

Scripture Reading: Romans 6:12-14
Focus Verse: Romans 6:13 (NASB)
"And do not go on presenting the members of your body
to sin as instruments of unrighteousness; but present
yourselves to God as those alive from the dead, and your
members as instruments of righteousness to God."

DEVOTION

Paul, a man who struggled with anger, would often find himself reacting in ways he regretted. After studying Romans 6:13, he decided to make a daily commitment: every morning, he prayed, "Lord, I present myself to You today as an instrument of righteousness." This simple act changed his perspective. "When I saw myself as God's instrument, I found it easier to respond with patience instead of anger," Paul shared.

Paul encourages us to make a conscious choice about how we use our bodies. Instead of letting sin control our actions, we are called to present ourselves to God as instruments of righteousness. This means we are to live intentionally, using our words, actions, and thoughts to glorify God rather than serve sin.

Presenting ourselves to God is an act of surrender, acknowledging that we belong to Him. It's a daily choice to live for God's purposes, allowing Him to work through us. This mindset transforms how we approach each day, helping us see every action as an opportunity to reflect Christ. When we present ourselves to God, we invite Him to use us as His vessels, bringing light and truth to the world.

FURTHER READING

Romans 12:1; 1 Corinthians 6:19-20; 2 Timothy 2:21

PRAYER

Father, I present myself to You today as an instrument of righteousness. Use my words, thoughts, and actions for Your glory. Help me to live each day fully surrendered to You. Amen.

CHALLENGE

Each morning, pray and dedicate yourself to God's service. Ask Him to guide you in being an instrument of righteousness and look for ways to show His love in your daily interactions.

DAY 6: SLAVES OF RIGHTEOUSNESS

Scripture Reading: Romans 6:15-18
Focus Verse: Romans 6:18 (NASB)
"And having been freed from sin, you be-
came slaves of righteousness."

DEVOTION

Steve had always thought freedom meant doing whatever he wanted, but he soon realized that following his desires often led to emptiness and regret. When he came across Romans 6:18, he understood a new kind of freedom, one where he was no longer bound by sin but free to serve righteousness. "I thought being free meant doing as I pleased," Steve reflected. "Now, I know true freedom is found in living for God."

Paul explains that we are freed from sin to become slaves of righteousness. While this language may seem counterintuitive, it captures a profound truth: true freedom is found in living according to God's will. Before Christ, we were enslaved to sin, unable to break free from its grip. But through Jesus, we are set free to live in a way that pleases God, fulfilling His purpose for our lives.

Being a "slave of righteousness" means that we are dedicated to living in obedience to God. This doesn't mean we lose our individuality; rather, we find our true purpose in aligning our lives with God's desires. When we embrace this freedom, we experience a life of purpose, joy, and fulfillment. Let's choose to live as slaves of righteousness, knowing that this is the path to true freedom.

FURTHER READING

John 8:36; Galatians 5:13; 1 Peter 2:16

PRAYER

Lord, thank You for setting me free from sin. Help me to live as a servant of righteousness, dedicated to Your will and purposes. May my life bring You glory. Amen.

CHALLENGE

Reflect on what it means to be a "slave of righteousness." In what areas of your life can you more fully surrender to God's will? Make a commitment to live in obedience to Him this week.

DAY 7: THE WAGES OF SIN IS DEATH

Scripture Reading: Romans 6:19-23
Focus Verse: Romans 6:23 (NASB)
"For the wages of sin is death, but the free gift of
God is eternal life in Christ Jesus our Lord."

DEVOTION

Lynn, a former addict, often shares her story of transformation. "I spent years working for sin, and all it brought me was emptiness and pain. But when I encountered God's grace, everything changed," she says. "I realized that God was offering me life as a free gift, and all I had to do was accept it. Looking back, I can see the truth of Romans 6:23: sin only brought death, but God's gift has given me true life."

Romans 6:23 presents a powerful contrast: the wages of sin is death, but God's gift is eternal life. Sin pays out in death, both physically and spiritually. It separates us from God, leaving us empty and without hope. But God, in His love, offers us a different outcome—a free gift of eternal life through Jesus Christ.

This verse reminds us that we don't have to work for God's gift. Unlike the consequences of sin, which are earned through our actions, eternal life is freely given to all who believe in Jesus. This truth should fill us with gratitude and humility, knowing that God's grace is unearned and undeserved. Let's embrace the life God offers, turning away from the wages of sin and stepping into the gift of life in Christ.

FURTHER READING

Ephesians 2:8-9; John 3:16; Titus 3:5-7

PRAYER

Father, thank You for offering me the gift of eternal life through Jesus. Help me to turn away from sin and embrace the life You have given me. May I live each day in gratitude for Your grace. Amen.

CHALLENGE

Reflect on the difference between the wages of sin and the gift of God. Share this truth with someone who may need to hear about the hope of eternal life.

WALKING FURTHER:
WEEK 8 QUESTIONS

1. What does it mean to be "dead to sin and alive in Christ"? How can this truth help you overcome temptation in your daily life?

2. How does understanding the significance of baptism deepen your relationship with God? In what ways does it encourage you to live as a new creation?

3. Reflect on what it means to be united with Christ in both His death and resurrection. How can this unity transform the way you view your identity?

4. What does it look like to "consider yourself dead to sin"? In what practical ways can you live this out each day?

5. How can presenting yourself to God each day as an instrument of righteousness shape the way you approach life?

6. What does true freedom look like as a "slave of righteousness"? How can you embrace this freedom more fully?

7. Romans 6:23 contrasts the wages of sin with the gift of eternal life. How does this truth impact the way you live and the way you share your faith?

WEEK 9: LIFE IN THE SPIRIT
(ROMANS 7-8)

THE STRUGGLE WITHIN
   – ROMANS 7:14-25

NO CONDEMNATION IN CHRIST
   – ROMANS 8:1-4

THE LAW OF THE SPIRIT
   – ROMANS 8:5-8

LED BY THE SPIRIT
   – ROMANS 8:9-14

THE SPIRIT OF ADOPTION
   – ROMANS 8:15-17

SUFFERING AND GLORY
   – ROMANS 8:18-25

THE SPIRIT INTERCEDES
   – ROMANS 8:26-27

DAY 1: THE STRUGGLE WITHIN

Scripture Reading: Romans 7:14-25
Focus Verse: Romans 7:19 (NASB)
"For the good that I want, I do not do, but I practice the very evil that I do not want."

DEVOTION

Tim, a dedicated Christian, often found himself frustrated by his own shortcomings. "I know what's right, and I want to do it, but I keep falling back into old habits," he confided to his friend. "I feel like I'm fighting an endless battle within myself." His friend shared with him this passage in Romans, and Tim was relieved to see that even Paul, the apostle, struggled with the same inner conflict.

Paul's honesty about his struggle with sin resonates with us because it's a battle every believer faces. Even as Christians, we are not immune to temptation and inner conflict. There's a war between our flesh—our old sinful nature—and the new life we have in Christ. Paul's words remind us that struggling doesn't mean we're failing in our faith; rather, it's a sign of our desire to live for God.

The struggle within is a reality, but we are not left to face it alone. While our flesh is weak, the Holy Spirit within us is strong. We must rely on His strength to resist temptation and to overcome our weaknesses. Acknowledging this struggle helps us lean on God's grace, knowing that even in our weakness, His grace is sufficient.

FURTHER READING

Galatians 5:17; Matthew 26:41; 2 Corinthians 12:9

PRAYER

Lord, thank You for understanding my struggles and for giving me the strength to overcome them. Help me to rely on Your grace and to walk in the Spirit, even in the face of my own weaknesses. Amen.

CHALLENGE

This week, whenever you feel the pull of your old nature, pause and pray. Ask the Holy Spirit to help you overcome the struggle within and to live in alignment with God's will.

DAY 2: NO CONDEMNATION IN CHRIST

Scripture Reading: Romans 8:1-4
Focus Verse: Romans 8:1 (NASB)
"Therefore there is now no condemnation for those who are in Christ Jesus."

DEVOTION

Lisa carried a deep sense of guilt over past mistakes, feeling as though she could never truly be forgiven. One day, a friend shared Romans 8:1 with her, explaining that in Christ, there is no condemnation. "It was like a weight lifted off my shoulders," Lisa shared. "I realized that Jesus had already taken my guilt, and I didn't need to carry it anymore."

Paul's statement in Romans 8:1 is incredibly freeing: in Christ, we are no longer condemned. Because of Jesus' sacrifice, the punishment for our sins has been fully paid. We are forgiven, accepted, and free to live without the burden of guilt or shame. This truth is essential to our identity as believers. No matter what we've done or how we've fallen short, Christ's forgiveness is complete, and His grace covers us.

When we understand that there is no condemnation in Christ, we can live in freedom, no longer weighed down by past mistakes. Let's embrace this truth and walk in the confidence that we are fully accepted and loved by God, not because of our perfection but because of Christ's perfect sacrifice.

FURTHER READING

John 3:17; Ephesians 1:7; Psalm 103:12

PRAYER

Lord, thank You for the freedom I have in Christ. Help me to live each day in the assurance that there is no condemnation for those who belong to You. Amen.

CHALLENGE

Whenever you feel weighed down by guilt or shame, remember Romans 8:1. Embrace the freedom that Christ has given you and refuse to let past mistakes define you.

DAY 3: THE LAW OF THE SPIRIT

Scripture Reading: Romans 8:5-8
Focus Verse: Romans 8:6 (NASB)
"For the mind set on the flesh is death, but the
mind set on the Spirit is life and peace."

DEVOTION

Carlos struggled with negative thoughts and anxieties that often overwhelmed him. When he learned about the "mind set on the Spirit" in Romans 8:6, he decided to make a change. "I began to pray and ask the Holy Spirit to guide my thoughts," Carlos said. "Over time, I noticed a peace that replaced the fear and negativity that used to control me."

Our thoughts have a powerful influence on our lives. When we set our minds on the desires of the flesh—our old sinful nature—it leads to anxiety, restlessness, and spiritual death. But when we set our minds on the Spirit, we experience life and peace. This is not something we achieve through sheer willpower; it's a transformation that happens when we invite the Holy Spirit to guide us.

Choosing to live by the "law of the Spirit" means letting the Holy Spirit shape our thoughts, attitudes, and actions. As we align our minds with God's truth, we experience a peace that goes beyond understanding. Let's make it a daily habit to seek the Spirit's guidance, setting our minds on Him and experiencing the life He offers.

FURTHER READING

Philippians 4:8-9; Isaiah 26:3; Colossians 3:2

PRAYER

Holy Spirit, help me to set my mind on You and to experience the life and peace You bring. Guide my thoughts and let them be filled with Your truth. Amen.

CHALLENGE

This week, whenever negative or anxious thoughts arise, pause and ask the Holy Spirit to guide your mind. Choose to set your thoughts on things that honor God and bring peace.

DAY 4: LED BY THE SPIRIT

Scripture Reading: Romans 8:9-14
Focus Verse: Romans 8:14 (NASB)
"For all who are being led by the Spirit of God, these are sons of God."

DEVOTION

Jamie was unsure about her next steps after finishing college. As she prayed, she remembered Romans 8:14 and asked God to lead her through His Spirit. "I didn't have all the answers right away, but I felt a peace and direction I couldn't explain," Jamie said. "Being led by the Spirit brought a calm that reassured me of God's plan."

One of the incredible privileges of being a child of God is that we are led by His Spirit. The Holy Spirit guides, comforts, and directs us, helping us make decisions and navigate life's uncertainties. When we yield to the Spirit's leading, we experience a sense of peace, knowing that God is with us every step of the way.

To be led by the Spirit means to trust in God's wisdom rather than our own. It requires humility and surrender, letting go of our plans and embracing His. As we listen to His guidance through prayer and the Word, we learn to follow His lead in every aspect of our lives. Let's cultivate a heart that seeks the Spirit's direction, confident that He will guide us in the path of God's will.

FURTHER READING

John 16:13; Psalm 143:10; Galatians 5:18

PRAYER

Lord, thank You for leading me by Your Spirit. Help me to be sensitive to Your guidance and to follow wherever You lead. Amen.

CHALLENGE

Spend time in prayer each day, asking the Holy Spirit to guide your steps. Look for His leading in both big decisions and small daily choices.

DAY 5: THE SPIRIT OF ADOPTION

Scripture Reading: Romans 8:15-17
Focus Verse: Romans 8:15 (NASB)
"For you have not received a spirit of slavery leading
to fear again, but you have received a spirit of adoption as sons by which we cry out, 'Abba! Father!'"

DEVOTION

Growing up, Caleb always felt alone and unwanted. When he became a Christian, he discovered the concept of adoption in Christ. "I
finally understood that God chose me to be His child," he shared. "Calling Him 'Father' made me feel loved and accepted in a way I had never
known."

As believers, we are adopted into God's family. We are no longer
slaves to fear, but children of God, with the privilege of calling Him
"Abba," which means "Father." This relationship is intimate and personal,
reflecting the deep love God has for us. Through the Spirit, we are assured
of our place in God's family, free from the fear and insecurity that once
bound us.

The Spirit of adoption reminds us that our identity is secure. We
belong to God, and nothing can separate us from His love. Let's live in
the confidence of being His children, knowing that we are fully accepted,
cherished, and loved by our heavenly Father.

FURTHER READING

Galatians 4:6-7; Ephesians 1:5; 1 John 3:1

PRAYER

Abba, Father, thank You for adopting me as Your child. Help me to
live in the security of being loved and accepted by You. Amen.

CHALLENGE

Reflect on what it means to be a child of God. Spend time thanking Him for adopting you into His family and living with the assurance of His love.

DAY 6: SUFFERING AND GLORY

Scripture Reading: Romans 8:18-25
Focus Verse: Romans 8:18 (NASB)
"For I consider that the sufferings of this present time are not worthy to be compared with the glory that is to be revealed to us."

DEVOTION

Anna, who faced years of chronic illness, clung to Romans 8:18 as her source of hope. "It reminded me that my suffering is temporary," she said. "One day, all the pain will be gone, and I'll see God's glory. That thought kept me going."

Paul encourages us to look beyond our present sufferings to the eternal glory awaiting us. Our trials may be intense, but they are temporary. God promises that what lies ahead will far outweigh the pain we experience now. As we fix our eyes on this hope, we find strength to endure, knowing that our future with God will be worth every hardship.

Let's hold on to this promise, trusting that God's glory will one day overshadow all our struggles. Our present pain is real, but it pales in comparison to the joy and peace we will experience in eternity.

FURTHER READING

2 Corinthians 4:17; Revelation 21:4; Hebrews 12:2

PRAYER

Father, thank You for the hope of glory that lies ahead. Help me to endure suffering with faith, trusting that one day, all pain will be gone and Your glory revealed. Amen.

CHALLENGE

Reflect on the hope of future glory. When you face challenges, remind yourself that God has prepared something far greater for you beyond this life.

DAY 7: THE SPIRIT INTERCEDES

Scripture Reading: Romans 8:26-27
Focus Verse: Romans 8:26 (NASB)
"In the same way the Spirit also helps our weakness; for we
do not know how to pray as we should, but the Spirit Himself intercedes for us with groanings too deep for words."

DEVOTION

When Sarah's father was diagnosed with a serious illness, she felt overwhelmed and didn't know how to pray. "I would sit in silence, not finding the right words," she said. "But then I remembered that the Holy Spirit prays for me, even when I can't. Knowing that brought me comfort and strength."

The Holy Spirit intercedes for us when we don't know how to pray. In our weakness, He speaks to the Father on our behalf, with groanings beyond words. This comforting truth reminds us that we are never alone, even in our hardest moments. The Spirit knows our hearts and prays according to God's will, bringing us peace and assurance.

Let's trust in the Spirit's intercession, knowing that He prays for us perfectly. When we feel lost or overwhelmed, we can rest, knowing that the Spirit is lifting us up, aligning our needs with God's perfect plan.

FURTHER READING

John 14:16-17; Ephesians 6:18; 1 John 5:14-15

PRAYER

Holy Spirit, thank You for interceding for me in my weakness. Help me to rely on Your strength, trusting that You know my needs and pray according to God's will. Amen.

CHALLENGE

When you're unsure how to pray, sit in God's presence and let the Spirit intercede. Trust that He understands your heart and prays on your behalf.

WALKING FURTHER:
WEEK 9 QUESTIONS

1. How does Paul's description of the "struggle within" encourage you in your own battles with sin? How can you rely on God's grace in those moments?

2. What does it mean for you to live without condemnation? How does this impact your relationship with God and others?

3. In what ways can you set your mind on the Spirit instead of the flesh? How might this choice impact your daily life?

4. How can you seek to be more sensitive to the Spirit's guidance in your decisions and actions?

5. What does it mean to you to be adopted as a child of God? How can this truth strengthen your faith?

6. How does the hope of future glory help you endure present sufferings? In what ways can you focus on this hope?

7. Reflect on the Spirit's role as an intercessor in your life. How does this comfort you during difficult times?

WEEK 10: GOD'S SOVEREIGN PURPOSE
(ROMANS 8:28-39)

ALL THINGS FOR GOOD
  – ROMANS 8:28-30

PREDESTINED FOR GLORY
  – ROMANS 8:29

WHO CAN BE AGAINST US?
  – ROMANS 8:31-34

HE GAVE HIS SON
  – ROMANS 8:32

MORE THAN CONQUERORS
  – ROMANS 8:35-37

NOTHING CAN SEPARATE US
  – ROMANS 8:38-39

MORE THAN WE ASK OR IMAGINE
  – ROMANS 8:32

DAY 1: ALL THINGS FOR GOOD

Scripture Reading: Romans 8:28-30
Focus Verse: Romans 8:28 (NASB)
"And we know that God causes all things to work together for good to those who love God, to those
who are called according to His purpose."

DEVOTION

After losing her job, Emma felt hopeless and anxious about her future. A friend reminded her of Romans 8:28, encouraging her to trust
God's purpose. Over time, Emma found a new job that not only provided for her but aligned more closely with her passions. "Looking back, I
see how God used that setback for good," she reflected. "He was working
in ways I couldn't see at the time."

Romans 8:28 is one of the most comforting promises in Scripture:
God is working all things together for our good. This doesn't mean everything we experience will feel good, but it assures us that God's purposes
are at work even in our trials. Our circumstances may be challenging, but
God's wisdom is greater, and He knows how to use every situation for our
growth and His glory.

When we trust that God is working for our good, we can face difficulties with hope. Instead of being discouraged by setbacks, we can
look for His hand at work, knowing that He sees the bigger picture. This
promise is for those who love God and are called according to His purpose. Let's hold on to this truth, believing that no matter what we face,
God is weaving it into His good plan.

FURTHER READING

Genesis 50:20; 2 Corinthians 4:17-18; James 1:2-4

PRAYER

Father, thank You for working all things together for my good. Help me to trust You, especially when I don't understand, and to believe that You are using every situation for my growth. Amen.

CHALLENGE

Think of a challenging situation you've faced. Reflect on how God may have used it for good, and thank Him for His faithfulness in every season.

DAY 2: PREDESTINED FOR GLORY

Scripture Reading: Romans 8:29
Focus Verse: Romans 8:29 (NASB)
"For those whom He foreknew, He also predestined
to become conformed to the image of His Son."

DEVOTION

Daniel, a new believer, was curious about God's plan for his life. As he read Romans 8:29, he was struck by the idea that God had predestined him to be like Christ. "It's amazing to think that God has been planning this all along," Daniel shared. "He's shaping me, even when I don't feel it."

God's plan for His children is nothing less than to be conformed to the image of His Son, Jesus. This process, called sanctification, is God's way of molding us to reflect His character. From the beginning, God's purpose has been to make us like Christ, and every experience, challenge, and blessing is part of that transformation.

This truth is comforting because it reminds us that our lives are not random; they are part of God's intentional design. He is actively working to shape us, and His purpose for us is glorious. Even when the journey is difficult, we can trust that He is fulfilling His plan to make us like Jesus.

FURTHER READING

Ephesians 1:4-5; 2 Corinthians 3:18; Philippians 1:6

PRAYER

Lord, thank You for Your purpose to make me more like Jesus. Help me to embrace Your work in my life and to yield to the process of becoming conformed to His image. Amen.

CHALLENGE

Reflect on an area of your life where God is shaping you to be more like Christ. How can you partner with Him in this transformation?

DAY 3: WHO CAN BE AGAINST US?

Scripture Reading: Romans 8:31-34
Focus Verse: Romans 8:31 (NASB)
"What then shall we say to these things? If
God is for us, who is against us?"

DEVOTION

After facing criticism at work, Laura felt discouraged and alone. A mentor reminded her of Romans 8:31, reassuring her that God was on her side. "I realized that no opposition could outweigh God's support," Laura shared. "If He's for me, that's all I need."

Application

Paul's words remind us of an empowering truth: if God is for us, no one can stand against us. This doesn't mean we won't face opposition or challenges, but it means that none of them can overpower the support of our Almighty God. Knowing that God is on our side gives us courage to face whatever comes our way, knowing that His power and love protect and sustain us.

When we feel overwhelmed by life's challenges, we can find confidence in the fact that God is with us. He is our defender, our refuge, and our strength. No accusation, trial, or hardship can separate us from His love. Let's hold onto this promise, standing firm in faith, knowing that God is always for us.

FURTHER READING

Psalm 27:1; Isaiah 41:10; 1 John 4:4

PRAYER

Father, thank You for being for me. Help me to stand firm in this truth, knowing that no challenge can overpower Your support and love. Amen.

CHALLENGE

When you face criticism or opposition this week, remind yourself of Romans 8:31. Let it strengthen your heart, knowing that God is with you.

DAY 4: HE GAVE HIS SON

Scripture Reading: Romans 8:32
Focus Verse: Romans 8:32 (NASB)
"He who did not spare His own Son, but delivered Him over for us all, how will He not
also with Him freely give us all things?"

DEVOTION

Steve often worried about whether God would provide for his family's needs. One day, he read Romans 8:32 and was struck by the truth
that if God gave His Son, He would surely meet every other need. "It put
everything in perspective," Steve reflected. "If God didn't hold back His
Son, I know He'll provide whatever we need."

God's gift of His Son is the ultimate expression of His love and generosity. If He was willing to give His very best—Jesus—to save us, we can
trust that He will provide everything else we need. God's provision isn't
limited; He freely gives us all things in Christ. This truth should give us
peace and confidence, knowing that our needs are secure in His hands.

Let's trust in God's generosity, confident that the One who gave us
His Son will provide for every need. When we remember the depth of
His love, we can rest in His care, knowing that He holds nothing back
from those who belong to Him.

FURTHER READING

John 3:16; Philippians 4:19; James 1:17

PRAYER

Lord, thank You for giving me Your Son. Help me to trust in Your
provision and to remember that You will freely give me all I need in
Christ. Amen.

CHALLENGE

Reflect on an area where you're struggling to trust God's provision. Surrender it to Him, remembering that He who gave His Son will provide for every need.

DAY 5: MORE THAN CONQUERORS

Scripture Reading: Romans 8:35-37
Focus Verse: Romans 8:37 (NASB)
"But in all these things we overwhelmingly conquer through Him who loved us."

DEVOTION

Rachel faced one hardship after another: job loss, health issues, and family struggles. Romans 8:37 reminded her that through Christ, she was more than a conqueror. "I realized I didn't have to be defined by my struggles," she said. "God's love made me victorious, even in my weakness."

Paul assures us that, through Christ's love, we are more than conquerors. This doesn't mean that we avoid hardship, but that we can rise above it. God's love empowers us to face life's challenges with confidence, knowing that nothing can defeat us when we stand in His strength.

Being more than a conqueror means that even in our weakness, God's power makes us victorious. We are not victims of our circumstances; we are overcomers because of Christ's love. Let's embrace this identity, facing each trial with courage, knowing that we are more than conquerors through Him.

FURTHER READING

1 John 5:4-5; 2 Corinthians 2:14; John 16:33

PRAYER

Lord, thank You for making me more than a conqueror through Your love. Help me to face every challenge with confidence, knowing that Your strength empowers me. Amen.

CHALLENGE

When facing difficulties this week, remind yourself that you are more than a conqueror. Let this truth strengthen you as you rely on God's love and power.

DAY 6: NOTHING CAN SEPARATE US

Scripture Reading: Romans 8:38-39
Focus Verse: Romans 8:39 (NASB)
"Nor height, nor depth, nor any other created thing, will be able to separate us from the love
of God, which is in Christ Jesus our Lord."

DEVOTION

Maria had gone through a painful divorce and felt utterly alone. When she read Romans 8:38-39, the assurance that nothing could separate her from God's love brought her comfort. "Even when I felt abandoned, I knew that God's love was holding me," Maria shared. "No circumstance, no loss could take that away."

Paul's declaration in Romans 8:38-39 is a powerful reminder of the unbreakable bond we have with God through Christ. No hardship, trial, or power (whether spiritual or physical) can separate us from His love. This truth is a source of hope, especially during life's most difficult moments, reminding us that we are never alone.

God's love is steadfast, enduring through every season and storm. This love is not based on our performance or circumstances; it's anchored in who God is and what Christ has done. No matter where we are or what we face, we can rest in the assurance that God's love is constant and unfailing.

FURTHER READING

Psalm 139:7-10; Jeremiah 31:3; Ephesians 3:18-19

PRAYER

Father, thank You for the unbreakable love You have for me in Christ. Help me to hold onto this truth, knowing that nothing can separate me from You. Amen.

CHALLENGE

When you feel distant from God, meditate on Romans 8:38-39. Let His love reassure you that He is with you, no matter what you're going through.

DAY 7: MORE THAN WE ASK OR IMAGINE

Scripture Reading: Romans 8:32
Focus Verse: Romans 8:32 (NASB)
"He who did not spare His own Son, but delivered Him over for us all, how will He not also with Him freely give us all things?"

DEVOTION

Jake often felt hesitant to ask God for help, thinking his needs were too small. But after reading Romans 8:32, he began to see God's generosity differently. "If God gave His Son for me, He won't withhold anything I need," Jake said. "I learned that I can come to Him with every need, big or small."

God's willingness to give His Son is the ultimate proof of His love and generosity. If He didn't hold back Jesus, we can be assured that He will provide all we need. This verse reminds us that God's resources and compassion are limitless. When we come to Him, we can trust that He not only hears our prayers but is ready to provide in ways beyond our expectations.

Our Heavenly Father delights in giving generously to His children. He is a God of abundance, willing to do more than we can ask or imagine. Let's approach Him with confidence, bringing our needs and desires, knowing that He loves us deeply and freely provides.

FURTHER READING

Ephesians 3:20-21; Matthew 7:11; 2 Corinthians 9:8

PRAYER

Lord, thank You for Your incredible generosity. Help me to trust You with my needs, knowing that You are always ready to give freely and abundantly. Amen.

CHALLENGE

Bring a need or desire before God in prayer this week, trusting that He can do more than you ask or imagine.

WALKING FURTHER:
WEEK 10 QUESTIONS

1. How does the promise that "all things work together for good" impact your perspective during trials?

2. What does it mean to you to be "predestined for glory"? How does this truth shape your view of God's plan for your life?

3. Reflect on the statement, "If God is for us, who can be against us?" In what ways can this give you courage and peace?

4. How does God's willingness to give His Son influence the way you trust Him for daily needs?

5. What does it mean to be "more than conquerors" through Christ? How does this impact how you approach life's challenges?

6. How does the assurance that nothing can separate you from God's love bring comfort in difficult times?

7. How can the knowledge that God can do "more than we ask or imagine" encourage you in your prayer life?

WEEK 11:
GOD'S SOVEREIGNTY
IN SALVATION
(ROMANS 9-10)

GOD'S SOVEREIGN CHOICE
– ROMANS 9:6-13

GOD'S MERCY AND COMPASSION
– ROMANS 9:14-18

THE POTTER AND THE CLAY
– ROMANS 9:19-24

A REMNANT CHOSEN BY GRACE
– ROMANS 9:25-29

STUMBLING OVER THE CORNERSTONE
– ROMANS 9:30-33

ZEAL WITHOUT KNOWLEDGE
– ROMANS 10:1-4

CONFESS AND BELIEVE
– ROMANS 10:5-13

DAY 1: GOD'S SOVEREIGN CHOICE

Scripture Reading: Romans 9:6-13
Focus Verse: Romans 9:11 (NASB)

"For though the twins were not yet born and had not done anything good or bad, so that God's purpose according to His choice would stand, not because of works but because of Him who calls."

DEVOTION

Tom often struggled to understand why God would choose one person over another. Reading about God's choice of Jacob over Esau, he found it hard to accept. But as he continued to study, he realized that God's choices are based on His purpose, not on human actions. "I saw that God's choice wasn't about merit but about His grace and purpose," Tom shared. "It humbled me to realize that my salvation is a result of His calling."

God's choice of Jacob over Esau reveals His sovereignty in salvation. Before they were born or had done anything good or bad, God chose Jacob. This passage reminds us that salvation is not earned by our actions but given by God's grace. His purposes are beyond our understanding, and He works according to His will, not our merit.

Understanding God's sovereign choice can be humbling and even difficult to grasp, but it also brings comfort. It reminds us that our salvation is secure because it is rooted in God's unchanging purposes, not our fluctuating actions. Let's embrace the truth of His sovereignty, resting in the assurance that He has chosen us and called us according to His purpose.

FURTHER READING

Ephesians 1:4-5; John 15:16; 2 Timothy 1:9

PRAYER

Father, thank You for choosing me according to Your purpose and grace. Help me to rest in Your sovereign choice and to trust that Your plans are good. Amen.

CHALLENGE

Reflect on the truth that your salvation is not based on your works but on God's calling. Let this bring you peace and gratitude today.

DAY 2: GOD'S MERCY AND COMPASSION

Scripture Reading: Romans 9:14-18
Focus Verse: Romans 9:15 (NASB)

"For He says to Moses, 'I will have mercy on whom I have mercy, and I will have compassion on whom I have compassion.'"

DEVOTION

Jenny, who had always believed that life was about earning what you receive, found it challenging to understand God's mercy. When she read Romans 9:15, she struggled with the idea that God's compassion isn't something we earn. "It was hard to let go of the idea of deserving, but I realized that mercy, by definition, can't be earned. It's a gift."

God's mercy and compassion are sovereign acts of His will, not rewards for our behavior. This truth reminds us that none of us can claim to deserve God's kindness. Instead, He chooses to extend mercy because it's in His nature. God's mercy is humbling because it reveals that salvation is an unearned gift, given out of His love and compassion.

This understanding of God's mercy should change how we relate to Him and others. Just as we have received mercy, we are called to extend mercy to those around us. Let's live with grateful hearts, acknowledging that our salvation is a result of God's compassion, not our works.

FURTHER READING

Exodus 33:19; Titus 3:5; Micah 7:18

PRAYER

Lord, thank You for Your mercy and compassion. Help me to live in gratitude for Your gift of salvation and to show mercy to others as You have shown it to me. Amen.

CHALLENGE

Think about someone who needs mercy in your life. Extend compassion toward them, remembering that God has shown you undeserved kindness.

DAY 3: THE POTTER AND THE CLAY

Scripture Reading: Romans 9:19-24
Focus Verse: Romans 9:21 (NASB)
"Or does not the potter have a right over the clay,
to make from the same lump one vessel for honorable use and another for common use?"

DEVOTION

Sarah loved making pottery and would spend hours molding clay into beautiful shapes. One day, as she read Romans 9:21, she realized that, like a potter with clay, God has the right to shape our lives as He sees fit. "It made me see that God is shaping me for His purposes, even when I don't understand," Sarah said. "I can trust Him as the potter of my life."

Just as a potter shapes clay according to his design, God has the right to shape our lives according to His purpose. This analogy reminds us of God's authority and sovereignty. Our lives are not accidents or random events; they are crafted by God's hands. He forms each of us with intention, creating us for specific purposes, whether honorable or humble.

Trusting God as the Potter means surrendering to His will, even when we don't understand His plans. We can rest in the assurance that He knows what He's doing and that His design is good. Let's embrace our role as clay in the Potter's hands, allowing Him to shape us according to His perfect purpose.

FURTHER READING

Isaiah 64:8; Jeremiah 18:6; 2 Timothy 2:20-21

PRAYER

Father, thank You for being the Potter of my life. Help me to trust Your hands and to submit to Your shaping, knowing that You are creating me for Your purpose. Amen.

CHALLENGE

Consider an area of your life where you've been resisting God's work. Surrender it to Him, trusting that He is the Potter, and His design is good.

DAY 4: A REMNANT CHOSEN BY GRACE

Scripture Reading: Romans 9:25-29
Focus Verse: Romans 9:27 (NASB)
"Isaiah cries out concerning Israel, 'Though the number of the sons of Israel be like the sand of the sea, it is the remnant that will be saved.'"

DEVOTION

Mark felt discouraged about the state of the world and the faith of those around him. When he read about the remnant in Romans 9, he was reminded that God always preserves a faithful few. "It helped me see that God's plan is still moving forward, even when it seems like only a few are following Him."

Throughout history, God has always preserved a remnant, a faithful few who remain devoted to Him. This remnant is chosen by grace, not because of their strength or numbers, but because of God's sovereign will. Even in times of widespread unbelief, God's purposes continue through those He calls.

The concept of a remnant chosen by grace should encourage us, especially when we feel like we're standing alone in our faith. God's work is not dependent on large numbers but on His power. Let's be part of His faithful remnant, trusting that His plans will prevail, even in difficult times.

FURTHER READING

Isaiah 10:22; Zechariah 13:8-9; Romans 11:5

PRAYER

Lord, thank You for preserving a faithful remnant by Your grace. Help me to stand firm in my faith, knowing that You are at work, even when the world around me seems far from You. Amen.

CHALLENGE

Pray for the strength to remain faithful, even when it feels like you're one of few. Trust that God's plans are moving forward, and you are part of His chosen remnant.

DAY 5: STUMBLING OVER THE CORNERSTONE

Scripture Reading: Romans 9:30-33
Focus Verse: Romans 9:33 (NASB)
"Just as it is written, 'Behold, I lay in Zion a stone
of stumbling and a rock of offense, and he who believes in Him will not be disappointed.'"

DEVOTION

When Paul's friend invited him to church, he initially resisted. He struggled with the message of the gospel, finding it hard to accept. But as he heard more about Jesus, he realized that what once seemed offensive was actually his source of salvation. "I had been stumbling over Jesus, but once I believed, everything changed."

Jesus is described as a cornerstone that some stumble over. For those who reject Him, He is a rock of offense; for those who believe, He is the foundation of salvation. This dual nature of Christ reveals the choice we all face: we can either reject Him or build our lives on Him.

Let's embrace Jesus as our cornerstone, trusting that He is the firm foundation upon which we can stand. Those who believe in Him will not be disappointed; rather, they will find strength, hope, and security in His love and grace.

FURTHER READING

Psalm 118:22; 1 Peter 2:6-8; Matthew 21:42

PRAYER

Lord, thank You for being the cornerstone of my life. Help me not to stumble over You but to build my life on Your unshakable foundation. Amen.

CHALLENGE

Reflect on what it means to have Jesus as the cornerstone of your life. Choose to build your actions, decisions, and identity on Him as your foundation.

DAY 6: ZEAL WITHOUT KNOWLEDGE

Scripture Reading: Romans 10:1-4
Focus Verse: Romans 10:2 (NASB)
"For I testify about them that they have a zeal for
God, but not in accordance with knowledge."

DEVOTION

Andrew had a passion for serving God, but he often relied on his own ideas rather than seeking God's wisdom. When he read Romans 10:2, he realized that zeal needed to be guided by knowledge of God's word. "I learned that passion isn't enough," he said. "I need to align my zeal with God's truth."

Zeal for God is a wonderful thing, but it must be guided by knowledge. Paul speaks about those who have enthusiasm for God but lack understanding, leading them down misguided paths. True zeal for God flows from a deep understanding of His Word and His will.

Let's strive to have both zeal and knowledge, seeking God's guidance in all we do. Passion alone can lead us astray, but when it's rooted in Scripture, it brings glory to God and fulfills His purposes.

FURTHER READING

Proverbs 19:2; Hosea 4:6; Philippians 1:9-11

PRAYER

Lord, give me both zeal and knowledge for You. Help me to seek Your truth and align my passion with Your will. Amen.

CHALLENGE

Evaluate where your zeal might be misguided. Ask God to help you align your enthusiasm with the wisdom and knowledge of His Word.

DAY 7: CONFESS AND BELIEVE

Scripture Reading: Romans 10:5-13
Focus Verse: Romans 10:9 (NASB)
"That if you confess with your mouth Jesus as
Lord, and believe in your heart that God raised
Him from the dead, you will be saved."

DEVOTION

When Julia heard the gospel for the first time, she was amazed by its simplicity. "All I had to do was confess Jesus as Lord and believe?" she thought. Taking that step of faith, she found peace and joy in salvation, grateful for the clear path to God that Scripture offered.

Paul's words in Romans 10:9 lay out the simplicity and power of salvation: confessing Jesus as Lord and believing in His resurrection. Salvation is not about complex rituals or impossible standards; it's about faith in Jesus Christ. Confessing Him as Lord is a declaration of His authority, and believing in His resurrection is a statement of trust in His victory over sin and death.

Let's remember that this confession and belief form the foundation of our relationship with God. They are not one-time actions but an ongoing expression of our faith and trust in Him.

FURTHER READING

John 3:16; 1 John 4:15; Acts 16:31

PRAYER

Lord Jesus, I confess You as my Lord and believe in Your resurrection. Thank You for the gift of salvation and for making a way for me to be with You. Amen.

CHALLENGE

If you've never publicly confessed Jesus as Lord, consider sharing your faith with someone this week. Embrace the joy and freedom that comes with professing your trust in Him.

WALKING FURTHER:
WEEK 11 QUESTIONS

1. How does the truth of God's sovereign choice affect your view of salvation?

2. Reflect on God's mercy and compassion. How does this shape your understanding of His character?

3. What does it mean for God to be the Potter and us the clay? How does this impact your response to His will?

4. How can the idea of a remnant chosen by grace encourage you in your faith?

5. In what ways is Jesus a "stone of stumbling" for some and a cornerstone for others? How has He been a cornerstone in your life?

6. Why is it important to have both zeal and knowledge in your relationship with God?

7. What does it mean to confess and believe in Jesus? How does this truth impact your daily walk with Him?

DR. RALPH W. JENKINS

WEEK 12: GOD'S FAITHFULNESS TO ISRAEL
(ROMANS 11)

HAS GOD REJECTED HIS PEOPLE?
– ROMANS 11:1-6

A REMNANT BY GRACE
– ROMANS 11:5-10

GRAFTED INTO THE OLIVE TREE
– ROMANS 11:11-24

DO NOT BE ARROGANT
– ROMANS 11:18-21

GOD'S KINDNESS AND SEVERITY
– ROMANS 11:22-24

THE MYSTERY OF GOD'S PLAN
– ROMANS 11:25-29

GOD'S GIFTS AND CALLING ARE IRREVOCABLE
– ROMANS 11:28-36

DAY 1: HAS GOD REJECTED HIS PEOPLE?

Scripture Reading: Romans 11:1-6
Focus Verse: Romans 11:1 (NASB)
"I say then, God has not rejected His people, has
He? May it never be! For I too am an Israelite, a de-
scendant of Abraham, of the tribe of Benjamin."

DEVOTION

Mark, who had felt distant from God after a season of doubt, wondered if God had given up on him. One day, he came across Romans
11:1 and was struck by Paul's assurance that God had not rejected His
people. "It gave me hope," Mark reflected. "If God remains faithful to
Israel, He'll remain faithful to me, even when I struggle."

Paul reassures the believers that God has not abandoned Israel. Even
though many Israelites rejected Jesus as Messiah, God's faithfulness to
His promises remains unshaken. This truth reminds us of God's character. He is a covenant-keeping God who remains loyal to His people, even
when they fall short.

Just as God did not reject Israel, He does not reject those who come
to Him in faith. Even when we experience seasons of doubt or struggle,
His commitment to us remains steadfast. Let's find comfort in God's
unchanging nature, trusting that He will never abandon those He has
chosen and called.

FURTHER READING

Psalm 94:14; Jeremiah 31:37; 1 Samuel 12:22

PRAYER

Lord, thank You for Your faithfulness to Israel and to all who trust in You. Help me to remember that You do not abandon Your people, even in times of doubt or struggle. Amen.

CHALLENGE

Reflect on a time when you felt distant from God. Consider how His faithfulness sustained you, and thank Him for His unwavering love.

DAY 2: A REMNANT BY GRACE

Scripture Reading: Romans 11:5-10
Focus Verse: Romans 11:5 (NASB)
"In the same way then, there has also come to be at the present time a remnant according to God's gracious choice."

DEVOTION

Sarah felt alone in her workplace, the only Christian among her colleagues. Romans 11:5 reminded her that God has always preserved a faithful remnant, even in difficult times. "Knowing that God keeps a remnant encouraged me to keep shining His light, even if I'm one of few," she said.

Throughout history, God has preserved a remnant of believers who remain faithful to Him. This remnant exists not because of their own strength or merit but because of God's grace. His choice to keep a remnant reflects His unwavering commitment to His promises and His people.

If you feel isolated in your faith, remember that God always has a remnant. You are not alone. Take courage from the knowledge that God is preserving you by His grace, and stay faithful to Him, even when the world around you seems distant from God.

FURTHER READING

1 Kings 19:18; Isaiah 10:21; 2 Timothy 1:9

PRAYER

Father, thank You for Your grace in preserving a remnant of believers. Help me to remain faithful, trusting that You are with me even when I feel alone. Amen.

CHALLENGE

If you feel isolated in your faith, seek out others who share your beliefs. Find encouragement in community and remember that you are part of God's remnant.

DAY 3: GRAFTED INTO THE OLIVE TREE

Scripture Reading: Romans 11:11-24
Focus Verse: Romans 11:17 (NASB)
"But if some of the branches were broken off, and you, being a wild olive, were grafted in among them and became partaker with them of the rich root of the olive tree."

DEVOTION

David, who had recently become a Christian, wondered if he truly belonged in God's family. When he read about being "grafted in" in Romans 11, he felt a sense of belonging. "I realized that God had welcomed me into His family and made me part of His promises," David shared.

The image of being grafted into the olive tree is a powerful reminder of God's grace and inclusion. Gentile believers are "wild branches" that have been grafted into the tree of Israel, becoming partakers of God's promises and blessings. This shows God's mercy and His desire to extend salvation to all people.

As grafted branches, we are called to honor our place in God's family. We are nourished by the same root, connected to the history and promises of Israel. Let's embrace our identity in Christ, rooted in God's family, and live in gratitude for the privilege of being grafted into His plan of salvation.

FURTHER READING

John 15:1-5; Ephesians 2:12-13; Galatians 3:14

PRAYER

Lord, thank You for grafting me into Your family. Help me to honor my place in Your kingdom and to live as one who is connected to Your promises. Amen.

CHALLENGE

Reflect on what it means to be grafted into God's family. Spend time thanking God for welcoming you into His kingdom and making you part of His promises.

DAY 4: DO NOT BE ARROGANT

Scripture Reading: Romans 11:18-21
Focus Verse: Romans 11:18 (NASB)
"Do not be arrogant toward the branches; but if you
are arrogant, remember that it is not you who supports the root, but the root supports you."

DEVOTION

After becoming a Christian, Amy noticed herself looking down on those who hadn't yet come to faith. Reading Romans 11:18 convicted her, reminding her that she was saved by grace, not by her own efforts. "I realized that I needed to stay humble, remembering that my faith is a gift," Amy shared.

Paul warns Gentile believers not to be arrogant toward Israel. Just as a branch cannot support the root, we cannot sustain ourselves spiritually. Our faith is rooted in God's promises and grace, not in anything we have done. This reminder calls us to humility, recognizing that we are recipients of God's mercy.

Let's guard our hearts against pride and self-righteousness, remembering that our place in God's family is a result of His kindness. Humility allows us to appreciate His grace and encourages us to extend that grace to others, inviting them to know Christ.

FURTHER READING

James 4:6; 1 Corinthians 4:7; Ephesians 2:8-9

PRAYER

Father, keep me humble, and help me to remember that my faith is a gift from You. May I never look down on others but extend Your grace to all. Amen.

CHALLENGE

Examine your heart for areas of pride in your faith. Ask God to help you stay humble, grateful for His mercy, and compassionate toward others.

DAY 5: GOD'S KINDNESS AND SEVERITY

Scripture Reading: Romans 11:22-24
Focus Verse: Romans 11:22 (NASB)
"Behold then the kindness and severity of God; to those who fell, severity, but to you, God's kindness, if you continue in His kindness; otherwise you also will be cut off."

DEVOTION

Tom, a new believer, found it difficult to reconcile the kindness and severity of God. When he read Romans 11:22, he began to understand that both aspects of God's character are essential. "God's kindness and His holiness go hand in hand," he realized. "His kindness saves us, but His holiness calls us to live faithfully."

Paul's words remind us that God's character includes both kindness and severity. He is merciful and loving, but He is also holy and just. While God extends kindness to those who believe, He also holds us accountable. This balance calls us to a life of reverence and gratitude, recognizing both His mercy and His justice.

Let's not take God's kindness for granted but respond with a heart that desires to please Him. His kindness leads us to repentance, and His severity reminds us of the importance of faithfulness. Let's hold both aspects of God's nature in awe, honoring Him with our lives.

FURTHER READING

Hebrews 12:28-29; Psalm 103:8; 1 Peter 1:17

PRAYER

Lord, thank You for Your kindness and Your holiness. Help me to honor both aspects of Your character, living a life that is grateful for Your mercy and reverent of Your holiness. Amen.

CHALLENGE

Reflect on how God's kindness and severity influence your faith. Allow His kindness to lead you to gratitude and His holiness to inspire faithful living.

DAY 6: THE MYSTERY OF GOD'S PLAN

Scripture Reading: Romans 11:25-29
Focus Verse: Romans 11:25 (NASB)
"For I do not want you, brethren, to be uninformed of
this mystery…that a partial hardening has happened to
Israel until the fullness of the Gentiles has come in."

DEVOTION

Mike had often wondered about God's plan for Israel and the world. When he read Romans 11:25, he realized that God's ways are mysterious but purposeful. "God's plan is greater than what I can see," Mike reflected. "He's working in ways I may not fully understand."

Paul speaks of a "mystery" in God's plan for Israel and the Gentiles. This mystery reveals God's wisdom and timing, as He works out His redemptive purposes for all people. While we may not understand every detail, we can trust that God's plan is perfect and that He is sovereignly at work.

Let's trust in the mystery of God's plan, knowing that He sees the whole picture. His timing and purposes are beyond our understanding, but we can rest in His faithfulness, knowing that His ways are good.

FURTHER READING

Isaiah 55:8-9; Ephesians 3:6; Colossians 1:26-27

PRAYER

Lord, thank You for Your wisdom and plan. Help me to trust in Your timing and purposes, even when I don't understand. Amen.

CHALLENGE

Reflect on a situation where you don't fully understand God's plan. Choose to trust in His wisdom, knowing that He is working all things together.

DAY 7: GOD'S GIFTS AND CALLING ARE IRREVOCABLE

Scripture Reading: Romans 11:28-36
Focus Verse: Romans 11:29 (NASB)
"For the gifts and the calling of God are irrevocable."

DEVOTION

After years of walking away from his faith, James felt unworthy to return to God. Reading Romans 11:29 reassured him that God's call on his life hadn't changed. "God hadn't given up on me, even when I'd walked away," James said.

God's gifts and calling are irrevocable. This truth reassures us that His promises are steadfast, and His calling on our lives remains, even when we fall short. God's faithfulness endures, and He is always ready to welcome us back.

Let's live in gratitude for God's unwavering promises, embracing His call and gifts with faith. His commitment to us is a source of strength and hope, reminding us that He is always faithful.

FURTHER READING

Psalm 89:34; 2 Timothy 2:13; 1 Peter 4:10

PRAYER

Thank You, God, for Your unchanging promises. Help me to walk faithfully in Your calling, grateful for Your steadfast love and faithfulness. Amen.

CHALLENGE

Reflect on the gifts and calling God has given you. Consider how you can honor His faithfulness by living out your calling.

WALKING FURTHER:

WEEK 12 QUESTIONS

1. How does God's faithfulness to Israel encourage you in your own relationship with Him?

2. Reflect on the concept of a remnant by grace. How can this encourage you when faith seems rare?

3. What does it mean to you to be "grafted" into God's family?

4. How does understanding God's kindness and severity impact the way you live out your faith?

5. What is one area where you need to trust God's mysterious plan?

6. How does knowing God's gifts and calling are irrevocable impact your confidence in His faithfulness?

7. In what ways can you show gratitude for being part of God's redemptive plan?

WEEK 13:
LIVING AS A SACRIFICE
(ROMANS 12:1-8)

A LIVING SACRIFICE
  – ROMANS 12:1

BE TRANSFORMED
  – ROMANS 12:2

HUMILITY IN SERVICE
  – ROMANS 12:3

ONE BODY, MANY MEMBERS
  – ROMANS 12:4-5

GIFTS OF GRACE
  – ROMANS 12:6-8

SERVING WITH DILIGENCE
  – ROMANS 12:7-8

LEADING WITH HUMILITY
  – ROMANS 12:8

DAY 1: A LIVING SACRIFICE

Scripture Reading: Romans 12:1
Focus Verse: Romans 12:1 (NASB)
"Therefore I urge you, brethren, by the mercies of God,
to present your bodies a living and holy sacrifice, acceptable to God, which is your spiritual service of worship."

DEVOTION

John had always thought of worship as something that happened only in church. But when he read Romans 12:1, he realized that true worship goes beyond Sunday mornings. "I began to see my whole life as an offering to God," John shared. "Every choice I make, every action, can be worship when I'm surrendered to Him."

Paul calls us to present our bodies as a "living sacrifice" to God. This means that our entire lives: our actions, thoughts, and attitudes are to be dedicated to God's service. Unlike the sacrifices in the Old Testament, which were dead offerings, we are called to be living sacrifices, continually offering ourselves to God.

Living as a sacrifice means surrendering our will and desires to God, choosing to honor Him in every aspect of our lives. It's a daily commitment to place God's purposes above our own, letting Him shape our lives. This is our spiritual worship—not confined to a church service but lived out every day in obedience to Him.

FURTHER READING

1 Corinthians 6:19-20; Galatians 2:20; Philippians 1:20-21

PRAYER

Lord, help me to live as a sacrifice, honoring You with every part of my life. May my thoughts, actions, and choices reflect my commitment to You. Amen.

CHALLENGE

Consider one area of your life where you can more fully surrender to God. Offer it to Him in prayer, asking for strength to live as a true living sacrifice.

DAY 2: BE TRANSFORMED

Scripture Reading: Romans 12:2
Focus Verse: Romans 12:2 (NASB)
"And do not be conformed to this world, but be transformed by the renewing of your mind, so that you may prove what the will of God is, that which is good and acceptable and perfect."

DEVOTION

Lisa had always struggled with self-doubt and negativity. When she came across Romans 12:2, she realized that God wanted to change the way she thought. "I used to let the world define my worth," she shared, "but now I'm learning to let God's truth shape my mind and my life."

Paul calls us to be transformed by the renewing of our minds. This transformation is not just about outward actions; it's about a complete change in the way we think. The world pressures us to conform to its standards, but God invites us to think and live according to His truth. Renewing our minds requires daily engagement with God's word, letting His truth reshape our thoughts, beliefs, and values.

When we allow God to renew our minds, we begin to see His will more clearly, understanding what is truly good and perfect. This transformation leads us to live in a way that honors God, making choices that align with His purposes.

FURTHER READING

Ephesians 4:23-24; Philippians 4:8; 2 Corinthians 10:5

PRAYER

Lord, help me to be transformed by the renewing of my mind. Let Your truth shape my thoughts, so I can live in a way that pleases You. Amen.

CHALLENGE

Choose one thought pattern you struggle with and seek to replace it with God's truth. Meditate on a verse that speaks to this area, allowing it to transform your perspective.

DAY 3: HUMILITY IN SERVICE

Scripture Reading: Romans 12:3
Focus Verse: Romans 12:3 (NASB)
"For through the grace given to me I say to everyone among you not to think more highly of himself than he ought to think; but to think so as to have sound judgment, as God has allotted to each a measure of faith."

DEVOTION

Michael, a leader in his church, was known for his dedication but often found himself feeling superior to others. Romans 12:3 challenged him to examine his heart. "I realized that pride was creeping in," he confessed. "God reminded me that my service should be marked by humility, not self-importance."

Paul encourages us to approach our service with humility, recognizing that every gift and ability comes from God. Pride can easily slip into our lives, especially when we're passionate about serving. But God calls us to think of ourselves with "sound judgment," understanding that we are all recipients of His grace.

Humility in service means acknowledging that our strength and abilities are gifts from God, given not for our glory but for His. When we serve with humility, we honor God and reflect His character to those around us. Let's strive to serve with a heart that values others, recognizing that we are all part of God's family and called to lift each other up.

FURTHER READING

Philippians 2:3-4; James 4:6; 1 Peter 5:5

PRAYER

Father, help me to serve with humility, recognizing that everything I have is a gift from You. Guard my heart against pride, and let my service reflect Your love. Amen.

CHALLENGE

Reflect on your attitude toward serving. If pride has crept in, ask God to replace it with humility, allowing you to serve others with a sincere heart.

DAY 4: ONE BODY, MANY MEMBERS

Scripture Reading: Romans 12:4-5
Focus Verse: Romans 12:5 (NASB)
"So we, who are many, are one body in Christ,
and individually members one of another."

DEVOTION

Samantha loved her role in the church choir, but she often felt that other ministries weren't as valuable. When she read Romans 12:5, she realized that every part of the body is essential. "I began to appreciate how God uses each person's unique gifts to build His church," she said. "We're all connected."

Paul's analogy of the church as a body reminds us that each member has a unique and important role. Just as a physical body needs all its parts to function, the church needs every person's gifts and contributions. No role is insignificant, and no member is unimportant.

Being part of one body means we're connected to each other, called to support, encourage, and value each person's contribution. Let's embrace our role within the body of Christ, appreciating the diversity of gifts that God has given to build His church.

FURTHER READING

1 Corinthians 12:12-27; Ephesians 4:16; Colossians 3:15

PRAYER

Lord, thank You for making me part of Your body. Help me to value others' gifts and to work together in unity, building up Your church. Amen.

CHALLENGE

Take time to thank someone who serves in a different role within the church. Encourage them in their unique calling and express gratitude for their part in the body of Christ.

DAY 5: GIFTS OF GRACE

Scripture Reading: Romans 12:6-8
Focus Verse: Romans 12:6 (NASB)
"Since we have gifts that differ according to the grace given to us, each of us is to exercise them accordingly."

DEVOTION

Anna often compared her gifts to others', feeling discouraged that she wasn't more talented in certain areas. When she read Romans 12:6, she realized that each gift is given by God's grace, not by personal merit. "It helped me accept and use the gifts God has given me, rather than wishing for someone else's."

Each of us has been given gifts according to God's grace. These gifts are diverse and reflect God's unique design for each person. Rather than comparing our gifts or downplaying our abilities, we're called to exercise our gifts faithfully, knowing that God has equipped us for specific purposes.

Using our gifts is an act of stewardship, honoring the grace God has given us. Let's embrace our unique callings and serve wholeheartedly, trusting that God's grace is sufficient for the work He has assigned to us.

FURTHER READING

1 Peter 4:10; 1 Corinthians 12:4-11; Ephesians 4:7

PRAYER

Thank You, Lord, for the gifts You have given me. Help me to use them faithfully, without comparing myself to others, trusting that Your grace is enough. Amen.

CHALLENGE

Identify one gift God has given you and find a way to use it to bless others this week. Embrace your calling, knowing that God has equipped you for His purposes.

DAY 6: SERVING WITH DILIGENCE

Scripture Reading: Romans 12:7-8
Focus Verse: Romans 12:7 (NASB)
"If service, in his serving; or he who teaches, in his teaching."

DEVOTION

After volunteering in the children's ministry, Carlos sometimes felt unappreciated and tired. But one Sunday, he read Romans 12:7 and realized that his service was ultimately for God. "When I saw it as serving Him, it renewed my strength and joy in what I was doing," he shared.

Paul encourages us to serve with diligence, recognizing that every act of service is an offering to God. Whether teaching, helping, or encouraging, each role within the church is valuable. Serving with diligence means committing ourselves wholeheartedly, even when the work is hard or unnoticed.

When we serve with a focus on God, our efforts become worship. Let's commit ourselves to diligent service, remembering that God sees and values every contribution, no matter how small.

FURTHER READING

Colossians 3:23-24; 1 Corinthians 15:58; Galatians 6:9

PRAYER

Father, help me to serve with diligence and joy, knowing that every act of service is for You. Strengthen me when I grow weary and let my work honor You. Amen.

CHALLENGE

Reflect on your attitude toward serving. Renew your commitment to serve with diligence, focusing on God's glory rather than human recognition.

DAY 7: LEADING WITH HUMILITY

Scripture Reading: Romans 12:8
Focus Verse: Romans 12:8 (NASB)
"He who leads, with diligence; he who
shows mercy, with cheerfulness."

DEVOTION

When Julia was promoted to a leadership position, she felt the pressure to prove herself. Reading Romans 12:8 reminded her to lead with humility and diligence, relying on God rather than her own abilities. "It shifted my focus from impressing others to serving them," she reflected.

Leading with humility means putting the needs of others above our own and serving with a heart that honors God. Paul reminds us to lead with diligence, not for our glory but for God's purposes. Leadership in the church is about serving and guiding others toward Christ, not seeking recognition or power.

Whether in formal roles or informal influence, we are all called to lead with humility. Let's follow Christ's example, leading others with a spirit of service and grace, pointing them toward God's love.

FURTHER READING

Matthew 20:26-28; 1 Peter 5:2-3; Philippians 2:3-4

PRAYER

Lord, help me to lead with humility and diligence, following Your example of servant leadership. May my influence bring others closer to You. Amen.

CHALLENGE

Reflect on a leadership role you have, whether formal or informal. Ask God to help you lead with humility, prioritizing others' needs above your own.

WALKING FURTHER:

WEEK 13 QUESTIONS

1. What does it mean to live as a "living sacrifice"? How can this shape your daily choices?

2. How can you renew your mind according to Romans 12:2? What steps can you take to align your thoughts with God's truth?

3. Why is humility important in service? How can you guard against pride as you serve?

4. What does it mean to be part of one body with many members? How does this impact your relationship with other believers?

5. Reflect on the gifts God has given you. How can you use them to serve His kingdom effectively?

6. What does serving with diligence look like for you? How can you renew your commitment to serve wholeheartedly?

7. How can you practice humility in leadership? What steps can you take to lead in a way that reflects Christ's example?

WEEK 14: LOVE IN ACTION
(ROMANS 12:9-21)

SINCERE LOVE
> – ROMANS 12:9

DEVOTED TO ONE ANOTHER
> – ROMANS 12:10

ZEALOUS IN SPIRIT
> – ROMANS 12:11

REJOICE IN HOPE
> – ROMANS 12:12

SHARING WITH OTHERS
> – ROMANS 12:13

BLESS THOSE WHO PERSECUTE YOU
> – ROMANS 12:14

REJOICE WITH THOSE WHO REJOICE
> – ROMANS 12:15

DAY 1: SINCERE LOVE

Scripture Reading: Romans 12:9
Focus Verse: "Love must be sincere. Hate
what is evil; cling to what is good."

DEVOTION

In a world filled with superficial connections, the call to sincere love challenges us to go deeper. Paul's words in Romans 12:9 remind us that true love isn't self-serving or conditional. Instead, it is genuine, honest, and rooted in a commitment to God's truth. It doesn't merely tolerate others but seeks their best interests with pure motives.

Sincere love begins with a heart transformed by Christ. When we encounter His sacrificial love, we are empowered to love others without hypocrisy. This kind of love goes beyond words; it is seen in actions that reflect God's goodness. Clinging to what is good means aligning our hearts and behaviors with God's standards, even when it requires us to stand against evil.

Jessica struggled to love a coworker who constantly undermined her efforts. One day, during her quiet time, she came across Romans 12:9. Convicted by the Holy Spirit, she began to pray for her coworker and look for ways to bless them. Over time, her actions softened their relationship, and Jessica experienced the freedom of loving sincerely, regardless of how she was treated.

When we allow God to fill our hearts with His love, our relationships are transformed. Sincere love enables us to forgive, bless, and walk in unity with others. It reflects the heart of God, drawing people closer to Him.

FURTHER READING:

John 13:34-35; 1 Corinthians 13:4-7

PRAYER

Lord, teach me to love sincerely. Help me to cling to what is good and hate what is evil. Fill my heart with Your love so that I may reflect Your goodness in my relationships. Amen.

CHALLENGE

Identify one relationship where you can practice sincere love. Take a practical step today to show God's love to that person.

DAY 2: DEVOTED TO ONE ANOTHER

Scripture Reading: Romans 12:10
Focus Verse: "Be devoted to one another in love.
Honor one another above yourselves."

DEVOTION

True devotion to others stems from the selfless love Christ modeled for us. In Romans 12:10, Paul calls believers to be deeply committed to one another, demonstrating love that prioritizes the needs of others over our own. This kind of devotion creates a community where people feel valued, supported, and encouraged in their faith journey.

Devotion requires intentionality. It's easy to care for those who reciprocate, but true devotion extends even to those who are difficult to love. Honor is a key part of this: treating others with respect and recognizing their worth as children of God. This kind of love strengthens the body of Christ and sets an example for the world.

Consider the story of Peter and Andrew, two men in their church small group. Peter had recently lost his job, and Andrew, though not well-off himself, went out of his way to encourage Peter, pray for him, and even offer practical help like meals and resume assistance. Their relationship grew as Andrew lived out Romans 12:10, honoring Peter's needs above his own comfort.

When we honor others, we reflect the humility of Christ, who didn't seek His own advantage but gave Himself for us. Devotion to one another goes beyond superficial acts. It's a lifestyle of love rooted in God's grace. As believers, we're called to build each other up and create a culture of care within the church.

FURTHER READING:

Philippians 2:3-4; John 15:12-13

PRAYER

Lord, help me to be devoted to others in love. Teach me to honor those around me and reflect Your selfless heart. Show me how to prioritize others in a way that glorifies You. Amen.

CHALLENGE

Look for a practical way to honor someone in your life today. It could be through a word of encouragement, an act of kindness, or simply listening with compassion.

DAY 3: ZEALOUS IN SPIRIT

Scripture Reading: Romans 12:11
Focus Verse: "Never be lacking in zeal, but keep
your spiritual fervor, serving the Lord."

DEVOTION

Passion is an unmistakable trait of someone who is devoted to a cause. In Romans 12:11, Paul encourages believers to maintain zeal and fervor in their service to the Lord. This isn't about fleeting enthusiasm or emotional highs, it's about a deep, abiding commitment that fuels our faith and energizes our actions for God's glory.

Zeal is more than just excitement; it's a reflection of our love for Christ. When we lose sight of our passion for God, our spiritual lives can become stagnant, and our service can feel like an obligation rather than a joy. Maintaining zeal requires staying connected to the source of our passion—Jesus Himself. Spending time in prayer, studying His Word, and serving others out of love rekindles the fire in our hearts.

Consider Mary, who served in her church's children's ministry for over 10 years. Over time, the routine began to feel like a chore. She prayed for renewal and was reminded of Romans 12:11. She realized that her work wasn't just about teaching, it was about planting seeds of faith in the next generation. Reframing her service as an offering to God restored her zeal and gave her a renewed sense of purpose.

To keep your spiritual fervor, focus on serving God with a grateful heart. Remember the eternal impact of your efforts, even when they feel small or unnoticed. Zeal isn't about being the loudest or most visible, it's about a quiet, steady devotion that honors the Lord.

FURTHER READING:

Colossians 3:23-24; Galatians 6:9

PRAYER

Lord, restore my passion for serving You. Help me to approach each task with joy and zeal, knowing that I'm working for Your glory. Keep my heart aligned with Your purpose. Amen.

CHALLENGE

Identify an area of ministry or service where you feel weary. Pray for renewed passion and look for ways to serve with fresh energy and commitment.

DAY 4: REJOICE IN HOPE

Scripture Reading: Romans 12:12
Focus Verse: "Be joyful in hope, patient in affliction, faithful in prayer."

DEVOTION

Hope is a powerful anchor for the soul. In Romans 12:12, Paul reminds us to rejoice in hope, even in the midst of challenges. This isn't a fleeting or shallow optimism; it's a deep, abiding confidence in God's promises. Hope looks beyond current circumstances to the eternal joy and peace found in Christ.

Rejoicing in hope requires shifting our focus from the temporary to the eternal. When trials come, it's easy to become discouraged or lose sight of God's goodness. But hope invites us to remember that God is faithful, His promises are true, and He is working all things for our good.

Consider Sarah, who faced a prolonged season of unemployment. There were moments when her faith wavered, but she clung to Romans 12:12, finding joy in the hope that God had a plan for her life. Through prayer and patience, she learned to trust in His timing. Eventually, she received a job offer that was far better than she had imagined. The journey taught her that God's hope is worth rejoicing in, even in the waiting.

Hope also strengthens us to endure affliction. When we trust in God's sovereignty, we can remain patient in trials, knowing that He is with us. Faithful prayer becomes our lifeline, connecting us to the source of hope and giving us strength to persevere.

FURTHER READING:

Psalm 33:20-22; Hebrews 6:19

PRAYER

Lord, thank You for the hope I have in You. Teach me to rejoice in Your promises, remain patient in trials, and stay faithful in prayer. Help me to reflect Your hope to those around me. Amen.

CHALLENGE

Think of an area in your life where hope feels distant. Write down a promise from God's word to meditate on this week, and rejoice in the hope it brings.

DAY 5: SHARING WITH OTHERS

Scripture Reading: Romans 12:13
Focus Verse: "Share with the Lord's people who are in need. Practice hospitality."

DEVOTION

Generosity is a tangible expression of God's love. In Romans 12:13, Paul calls believers to share with those in need and to practice hospitality. These actions go beyond meeting physical needs—they demonstrate the heart of Christ to a watching world.

Sharing with others begins with recognizing that all we have comes from God. When we view our resources as blessings entrusted to us by Him, we're more willing to give freely. Generosity doesn't depend on the amount we give but on the heart with which we give. Even small acts of kindness can have a profound impact.

Consider Mark and Lisa, who hosted a struggling young couple in their church. Despite having limited resources themselves, they opened their home and shared what they had. Their simple hospitality not only met a practical need but also showed the couple what it meant to live out God's love.

Hospitality isn't just about opening your home—it's about opening your heart. It's an intentional effort to create a space where others feel welcome, valued, and cared for. Whether it's through a meal, a kind word, or a helping hand, practicing hospitality reflects the character of Christ.

God's word reminds us that when we serve others, we are serving Him (Matthew 25:40). By sharing what we have and extending hospitality, we participate in God's work of meeting needs and transforming lives.

FURTHER READING:

1 Peter 4:9-10; Proverbs 19:17

PRAYER

Father, thank You for blessing me with what I have. Teach me to be generous with my resources and my time. Help me to share with those in need and practice hospitality with joy. Amen.

CHALLENGE

Identify someone in your life who is in need—physically, emotionally, or spiritually. Find a practical way to share with them this week, whether through a meal, encouragement, or prayer.

DAY 6: BLESS THOSE WHO PERSECUTE YOU

Scripture Reading: Romans 12:14
Focus Verse: "Bless those who persecute you; bless and do not curse."

DEVOTION

Loving those who treat us well is easy. Blessing those who persecute us, however, requires a supernatural strength that only God can provide. Romans 12:14 challenges us to respond to mistreatment not with retaliation, but with blessing—a reflection of God's grace working through us.

Jesus modeled this perfectly. On the cross, He prayed, *"Father, forgive them, for they do not know what they are doing"* (Luke 23:34). This act of grace and mercy exemplifies the radical love God calls us to extend to others, even to our enemies.

Consider Aaron, a high school teacher who faced constant criticism from a colleague. His initial reaction was frustration, but as he meditated on Romans 12:14, he realized that God was calling him to bless this person instead of harboring resentment. Aaron began praying for his colleague daily and found his heart softening. Over time, their relationship improved, and Aaron experienced the freedom that comes from releasing bitterness.

Blessing those who persecute us doesn't mean approving of their actions or allowing harm to continue. It means choosing forgiveness and seeking God's best for them through prayer and grace. This doesn't just change the other person—it transforms our hearts as well.

When we bless instead of curse, we reflect God's love in a world that desperately needs it. We show that His grace is greater than any offense and that His love can overcome even the deepest wounds.

FURTHER READING:

Matthew 5:44; 1 Peter 3:9

PRAYER

Lord, help me to bless those who mistreat me. Teach me to respond with love and grace, trusting You to work in their hearts. Free me from bitterness and fill me with Your peace. Amen.

CHALLENGE

Think of someone who has mistreated or wronged you. Pray for them this week, asking God to bless them and transform both your hearts.

DAY 7: REJOICE WITH THOSE WHO REJOICE

Scripture Reading: Romans 12:15
Focus Verse: "Rejoice with those who rejoice; mourn with those who mourn."

DEVOTION

Celebrating the joys of others seems simple, but true rejoicing requires a heart free of envy and comparison. Romans 12:15 calls us to share in the happiness of others with genuine love and enthusiasm, reflecting God's selfless care for His people.

In a world driven by achievement and recognition, it can be challenging to rejoice with others when we're facing our own struggles. Yet, Paul's command reminds us that love seeks the good of others, finding joy in their blessings and successes. When we set aside our pride and envy, we create space for genuine celebration that builds unity and deepens relationships.

Megan had always dreamed of starting her own business, but financial struggles delayed her plans. When her best friend Sarah shared that she had launched a thriving boutique, Megan initially felt a pang of jealousy. But as she prayed and meditated on Romans 12:15, she realized that her role as a friend was to celebrate Sarah's success, not compare it to her own situation. Megan chose to support Sarah wholeheartedly, and their friendship grew stronger as a result.

Rejoicing with others isn't just about sharing in their happiness—it's about reflecting God's heart. He delights in blessing His children and calls us to share in that delight. This kind of rejoicing strengthens the body of Christ, encouraging one another and fostering an environment of love and gratitude.

When we rejoice with those who rejoice, we build a community of support and encouragement that glorifies God and draws others closer to Him.

FURTHER READING:
Philippians 2:3-4; 1 Thessalonians 5:16-18

PRAYER
Lord, teach me to rejoice with those who rejoice. Help me to celebrate the blessings of others with a sincere and loving heart. Free me from envy, and fill me with gratitude for all You have done. Amen.

CHALLENGE
Identify someone who is celebrating a milestone or success. Take time to genuinely rejoice with them—send a message, give a gift, or offer encouragement

WALKING FURTHER:
WEEK 14 QUESTIONS

1. How can you practice sincere love toward others in your daily life?

2. What steps can you take to be more devoted to others in your church or community?

3. Reflect on what it means to serve the Lord with a fervent spirit. How can you keep this enthusiasm in your walk with God?

4. In what ways does hope help you persevere in difficult times?

5. Consider how you can share and show hospitality to others this week.

6. Who is someone you can pray for, even if they have been challenging to you?

7. How can you actively rejoice with others and show empathy in their moments of joy or sadness?

WEEK 15: OVERCOMING EVIL WITH GOOD
(ROMANS 12:16-21)

LIVING IN HARMONY
- ROMANS 12:16

HUMILITY TOWARD OTHERS
- ROMANS 12:16

DO WHAT IS HONORABLE
- ROMANS 12:17

LIVE AT PEACE WITH EVERYONE
- ROMANS 12:18

VENGEANCE IS GOD'S
- ROMANS 12:19

DO NOT BE OVERCOME BY EVIL
- ROMANS 12:20-21

OVERCOME EVIL WITH GOOD
- ROMANS 12:21

DAY 1: LIVE IN HARMONY

Scripture Reading: Romans 12:16
Focus Verse: *"Live in harmony with one another. Do not be proud, but be willing to associate with people of low position. Do not be conceited."*

DEVOTION

Harmony requires intentionality. Paul's instruction to "live in harmony with one another" highlights the need for unity among believers, regardless of differences. True harmony involves humility and a willingness to value others above ourselves.

Pride often disrupts harmony. When we elevate our opinions or status above others, it creates division. Paul reminds us not to be conceited but to associate with people from all walks of life. Jesus exemplified this humility when He spent time with tax collectors, fishermen, and the marginalized, showing that His love extended to everyone.

Consider Alex, a successful business owner who initially avoided volunteering at his church's outreach ministry, feeling it wasn't a good use of his skills. When he finally joined, he worked alongside people from different backgrounds and realized how much he could learn from their perspectives. Through this experience, Alex grew in humility and built relationships that reflected God's love.

Living in harmony doesn't mean avoiding conflict or ignoring differences. It means approaching relationships with grace, humility, and a desire for unity. When we reflect Christ's humility, we foster peace and build a community that glorifies Him.

FURTHER READING:

Philippians 2:3-5; Colossians 3:12-14

PRAYER

Lord, help me to live in harmony with others. Teach me to value humility over pride and unity over division. Let my actions reflect Your love and grace. Amen.

CHALLENGE

Think of a relationship where pride or misunderstanding has caused division. Take one step today to restore harmony, whether through a conversation or an act of kindness.

DAY 2: DO NOT REPAY EVIL FOR EVIL

Scripture Reading: Romans 12:17
Focus Verse: "Do not repay anyone evil for evil. Be careful to do what is right in the eyes of everyone."

DEVOTION

The natural response to being wronged is often to seek revenge, but God calls us to a higher standard. Romans 12:17 instructs us not to repay evil for evil but to act with integrity, reflecting Christ's character even in difficult situations.

Retaliation only perpetuates conflict. By refusing to repay evil, we break the cycle of hurt and open the door for reconciliation. Instead of reacting in anger, we are called to do what is right—acting with kindness, forgiveness, and self-control.

Karen was deeply hurt when a coworker spread false rumors about her. She felt justified in confronting the coworker harshly but instead chose to follow Paul's advice in Romans 12:17. She prayed for wisdom and responded calmly, refusing to retaliate. Over time, her integrity won the respect of her team and even softened her coworker's attitude.

Living this way requires strength from the Holy Spirit. Our own efforts may falter, but God empowers us to choose grace over retaliation. By doing so, we reflect the heart of Christ, who forgave His enemies even as He suffered on the cross.

FURTHER READING:

Matthew 5:38-39; 1 Peter 3:9

PRAYER

Lord, help me to respond to wrongdoing with grace and integrity. Teach me to trust You to bring justice in Your time. Amen.

CHALLENGE

Identify a situation where you've been tempted to retaliate. Choose to respond with kindness and prayer instead of anger.

DAY 3: LIVE PEACEFULLY WITH ALL

Scripture Reading: Romans 12:18
Focus Verse: "If it is possible, as far as it depends on you, live at peace with everyone."

DEVOTION

Peace doesn't happen by accident. Paul's words in Romans 12:18 emphasize that believers should strive for peace with everyone, as far as it depends on us. This requires effort, humility, and a commitment to letting go of offenses.

Living peacefully doesn't mean compromising truth or avoiding conflict at all costs. It means approaching disagreements with a heart of love and a desire for resolution. Peace reflects God's character and points others to the Prince of Peace, Jesus Christ.

Mike struggled with a neighbor who constantly complained about his dog barking. Frustrated, Mike wanted to ignore the issue, but he prayed for wisdom and decided to have a calm conversation. By listening to his neighbor's concerns and working toward a solution, Mike was able to restore peace to their relationship.

Sometimes, despite our best efforts, others may refuse to live peacefully with us. We can rest in these moments, knowing that we've done our part, trusting God to handle the rest.

FURTHER READING:

Matthew 5:9; Hebrews 12:14

PRAYER

Father, help me to be a peacemaker in my relationships. Teach me to seek resolution and to reflect Your love in all situations. Amen.

CHALLENGE

Consider a relationship where peace is lacking. Take one intentional step today to pursue reconciliation, whether through a conversation, prayer, or a gesture of kindness

DAY 4: LEAVE ROOM FOR GOD'S WRATH

Scripture Reading: Romans 12:19
Focus Verse: "Do not take revenge, my dear friends,
but leave room for God's wrath, for it is written: 'It
is mine to avenge; I will repay,' says the Lord."

DEVOTION

Revenge feels like justice, but God reminds us in Romans 12:19 that vengeance belongs to Him alone. Taking matters into our own hands often leads to bitterness and broken relationships. When we surrender our desire for revenge, we trust God to act in His perfect timing and justice.

David's story with King Saul is a powerful example of leaving vengeance to God. Though Saul sought to kill him, David refused to harm God's anointed. Instead, he trusted God to handle the situation. David's restraint demonstrated his faith in God's sovereignty, and in time, God dealt with Saul.

Leaving room for God's wrath doesn't mean ignoring wrongdoing. It means choosing forgiveness and trusting God to bring about justice. Revenge seeks immediate satisfaction, but God's justice is eternal and perfect.

Consider Linda, who faced betrayal from a close friend. Her initial reaction was to confront the friend angrily, but she chose to pray instead. Through prayer, Linda found peace, letting go of her anger and trusting God to handle the situation. Though reconciliation didn't come immediately, Linda experienced freedom from bitterness.

FURTHER READING:

Proverbs 20:22; Matthew 5:44

PRAYER

Lord, help me to trust You with justice. Teach me to release my desire for revenge and to forgive those who have wronged me. Amen.

CHALLENGE

Identify a situation where you've been holding onto a desire for revenge. Pray for the strength to surrender it to God and trust in His justice.

DAY 5: FEED YOUR ENEMY

Scripture Reading: Romans 12:20
Focus Verse: "If your enemy is hungry, feed him;
if he is thirsty, give him something to drink. In doing this, you will heap burning coals on his head."

DEVOTION

Loving an enemy is one of the most challenging commands in Scripture. Yet Romans 12:20 calls us to respond to hostility with kindness,
reflecting God's radical grace. By feeding our enemies and meeting their
needs, we demonstrate a love that goes beyond human understanding.

This command isn't about passive acceptance of wrongdoing. It's
about actively choosing to bless others, even those who oppose us. When
we respond to hatred with love, we reveal the heart of God and pave the
way for potential reconciliation.

Tom had a neighbor who constantly criticized his landscaping. Instead of retaliating, Tom decided to invite his neighbor over for coffee.
Though awkward at first, the gesture softened their relationship. Tom's
kindness opened the door for conversations about faith, eventually leading his neighbor to Christ.

The phrase "heap burning coals" isn't about causing harm; it signifies
convicting someone through unexpected love. When we act with kindness, it often surprises our enemies and may lead them to repentance.

FURTHER READING:
Luke 6:27-28; Proverbs 25:21-22

PRAYER

Father, teach me to love my enemies as You love them. Help me to
respond with kindness and grace, trusting You to work in their hearts.
Amen.

CHALLENGE

Identify someone who has wronged or opposed you. Take a specific action this week to bless them, such as offering a kind word or meeting a need.

DAY 6: OVERCOME EVIL WITH GOOD

Scripture Reading: Romans 12:21
Focus Verse: "Do not be overcome by evil,
but overcome evil with good."

DEVOTION

Evil often feels overwhelming, but Romans 12:21 calls believers to a higher standard: overcome it with good. This is not about ignoring evil but about actively resisting it through godly actions and attitudes.

Jesus overcame the evil of sin and death through His sacrificial love. His victory sets the example for us to follow, showing that love, kindness, and truth are far more powerful than hate and revenge.

Jessica faced a difficult work environment where gossip and negativity were rampant. Instead of joining in, she chose to speak positively and encourage her coworkers. Over time, her example influenced others, and the workplace culture began to change.

Overcoming evil with good requires courage and faith. It's not always easy, but God equips us with His Spirit to live out this calling. Each act of goodness reflects His glory and pushes back the darkness.

FURTHER READING:

Galatians 6:9-10; 1 Thessalonians 5:15

PRAYER

Lord, give me the strength to overcome evil with good. Help me to shine Your light in dark places and to trust in Your victory. Amen.

CHALLENGE

Think of an area in your life where evil seems to prevail. Commit to responding with goodness this week, trusting God to use your actions for His glory.

DAY 7: LIVING IN TRUE HUMILITY

Scripture Reading: Romans 12:16
Focus Verse: "Do not be proud, but be willing to associate with people of low position. Do not be conceited."

DEVOTION

Humility is foundational to living a Christ-centered life. In Romans 12:16, Paul challenges believers to abandon pride, embrace humility, and treat others with dignity and respect, regardless of their social or economic status. True humility reflects the heart of Christ, who humbled Himself to serve and save us.

Pride creates barriers, while humility builds bridges. When we think too highly of ourselves, we lose sight of our dependence on God and the value He places on others. Humility reminds us that all we have is a gift from Him and that every person is created in His image.

Rebecca, a successful lawyer, initially resisted mentoring at a local youth center, thinking her time was better spent elsewhere. But when she took the step, she realized how much she could learn from the young people she mentored. Their resilience and faith inspired her, and she saw how serving others deepened her walk with God.

Humility is not thinking less of yourself but thinking of yourself less. It shifts the focus from self-promotion to serving others with love. Jesus exemplified this in John 13 when He washed the feet of His disciples—a task reserved for servants. His humility calls us to follow His example in our daily lives.

Living in humility glorifies God and unites His people. It allows us to love sincerely, serve selflessly, and reflect the character of Christ to a watching world.

FURTHER READING:

Philippians 2:5-8; Micah 6:8

PRAYER

Lord, help me to live in humility. Teach me to value others as You value them and to serve with a heart that reflects Your love. Strip away my pride and fill me with Your grace. Amen.

CHALLENGE

Identify an act of humility you can practice this week. Whether it's serving someone in need or seeking reconciliation in a strained relationship, commit to following Christ's example of humble love.

WALKING FURTHER:

WEEK 15 QUESTIONS

1. How can you live in harmony with others this week, fostering peace in your relationships?

2. What does humility toward others look like in your daily life?

3. Reflect on a time when responding honorably made a difference in a conflict. How can this guide you in the future?

4. Why is pursuing peace with others important in your witness for Christ?

5. In what situation do you need to trust God with justice, rather than seeking revenge?

6. How does responding to negativity with kindness reflect Christ's love?

7. How can you overcome evil with good in a specific area of your life this week?

WEEK 16: SUBMITTING TO AUTHORITY AND LOVE FULFILLS THE LAW
(ROMANS 13)

SUBMIT TO AUTHORITIES
   – ROMANS 13:1-2

LIVING UNDER AUTHORITY
   – ROMANS 13:3-5

RENDER TO ALL WHAT IS DUE
   – ROMANS 13:6-7

THE DEBT OF LOVE
   – ROMANS 13:8

LOVE FULFILLS THE LAW
   – ROMANS 13:9-10

THE DAY IS NEAR
   – ROMANS 13:11-12

LET US BEHAVE PROPERLY
   - ROMANS 13:13-14

DAY 1: SUBMIT TO AUTHORITIES

Scripture Reading: Romans 13:1-2
Focus Verse: "Let everyone be subject to the governing authorities, for there is no authority except that which God has established. The authorities that exist have been established by God."

DEVOTION

Submission is a challenging concept, especially in a world where authority is often misused. Yet Romans 13:1-2 reminds us that all authority is established by God. This doesn't mean every leader is perfect or godly, but it does mean that God is sovereign over the institutions of authority.

Paul wrote these words during a time of Roman rule, when Christians faced persecution and injustice. His call to submit wasn't about blind obedience but about honoring God by respecting the order He has established. Submission reflects trust in God's sovereignty, even when we don't fully understand His plan.

Jessica struggled with a difficult boss who often criticized her work unfairly. Instead of responding with resentment, she prayed for her boss and sought to maintain a respectful attitude. Over time, her humility and diligence softened their relationship, showing her boss a glimpse of God's grace.

Submitting to authorities doesn't mean compromising our faith or condoning wrongdoing. When authority conflicts with God's commands, we are called to obey God above all (Acts 5:29). However, in matters that don't contradict His Word, we honor Him by respecting the authority He has placed over us.

Ultimately, submission is about trusting God's sovereignty. When we respect those in authority, we reflect His order and His glory, pointing others to the ultimate authority—Jesus Christ.

FURTHER READING:
1 Peter 2:13-15; Titus 3:1

PRAYER
Lord, help me to honor the authorities You've placed in my life. Teach me to trust in Your sovereignty and to reflect Your grace in my actions. Amen.

CHALLENGE
Identify an authority figure in your life who has been challenging to respect. Commit to praying for them daily this week and look for ways to show humility and honor.

DAY 2: LIVING UNDER AUTHORITY (EXPANDED)

Scripture Reading: Romans 13:3-5
Focus Verse: "For rulers hold no terror for those
who do right, but for those who do wrong. Do
what is right and you will be commended."

DEVOTION

Authority is designed by God to promote order, justice, and peace. In Romans 13:3-5, Paul explains that rulers are meant to commend those who do right and punish those who do wrong. When we live according to God's ways, we align ourselves with His design for authority and reflect His righteousness.

This passage doesn't suggest that all authorities are perfect, but it does remind us that doing right often leads to peace and favor. Living under authority with integrity protects us from unnecessary conflict and positions us as examples of Christ's character. Even when authority is flawed, our response should reflect God's heart.

Mike, a delivery driver, was once given a speeding ticket while rushing to complete his route. Frustrated, he wanted to argue the fairness of the law. However, after reading Romans 13, he realized that obeying speed limits wasn't just about avoiding punishment—it was about honoring God by respecting the laws in place. From that day forward, Mike committed to driving responsibly as a way to glorify God.

Living under authority requires humility and self-discipline. When we honor the laws and leaders in our lives, we reflect trust in God's order. This doesn't mean ignoring injustice; it means living in a way that demonstrates respect and obedience to God's principles.

This extends to daily interactions with supervisors, government laws, or even family roles. The goal isn't perfection, but a heart aligned with God's word, striving to honor Him in how we live.

FURTHER READING:
Proverbs 21:1; Ecclesiastes 8:2-5

PRAYER
Father, teach me to live under authority with integrity and humility. Help me to honor You in how I obey the laws and respect the leaders You've placed in my life. Amen.

CHALLENGE
Examine an area in your life where you struggle to follow authority. Take a step this week to align your actions with God's design for obedience.

DAY 3: RENDER TO ALL WHAT IS DUE

Scripture Reading: Romans 13:6-7
Focus Verse: "This is also why you pay taxes, for the authorities are God's servants, who give their full time to governing. Give to everyone what you owe them: If you owe taxes, pay taxes; if revenue, then revenue; if respect, then respect; if honor, then honor."

DEVOTION

Paying taxes may not seem like a spiritual act, but Romans 13:6-7 reminds us that it is part of honoring God's authority. Paul teaches that governing authorities are servants of God, and by fulfilling our obligations—whether financial, legal, or relational—we demonstrate trust in God's sovereignty.

Rendering what is due goes beyond taxes. It includes showing respect and honor to leaders and those in positions of authority. This can be difficult, especially when we disagree with their decisions, but our attitude reflects our relationship with Christ. Respect doesn't mean blind agreement; it means choosing to act with integrity and humility.

Consider Daniel, who served under foreign kings in Babylon. Though these rulers didn't follow God, Daniel fulfilled his duties with excellence and showed respect, earning favor while remaining faithful to God. His life demonstrated how honoring authority can bring glory to God.

When we render what is due, we witness to the world that our hope is not in earthly systems but in God's eternal kingdom. By honoring others, we point to the One who deserves ultimate honor and praise.

FURTHER READING:

Matthew 22:21; 1 Peter 2:17

PRAYER

Lord, help me to give what is due with a willing heart. Teach me to show respect, honor, and integrity in all my interactions. Let my actions reflect my trust in You. Amen.

CHALLENGE

Reflect on an area where you've struggled to fulfill your obligations—financially, relationally, or otherwise. Take steps this week to render what is due as an act of obedience to God.

DAY 4: THE DEBT OF LOVE

Scripture Reading: Romans 13:8
Focus Verse: "Let no debt remain outstanding, except the continuing debt to love one another, for whoever loves others has fulfilled the law."

DEVOTION

Love is the only debt that can never be fully repaid. Romans 13:8 teaches us to live free of financial and relational debts, except for the ongoing call to love one another. This debt isn't a burden but a privilege—it reflects the love Christ has poured out on us.

Paul reminds us that loving others fulfills the law because love encompasses all that God commands. When we love, we naturally seek the good of others, avoid harm, and reflect God's character. This love is not based on feelings or convenience; it's a deliberate choice to put others' needs above our own.

Jenna struggled with resentment toward a coworker who often took credit for her work. But as she meditated on Romans 13:8, she felt convicted to respond with love rather than bitterness. She began praying for her coworker and looked for ways to encourage them. Over time, Jenna found freedom in letting love guide her actions instead of resentment.

The "debt of love" isn't something we can repay on our own. It flows from the love God has shown us through Christ. His sacrifice enables us to love others selflessly and consistently, even when it's difficult.

Living out this love transforms relationships and points others to Jesus. It breaks down barriers, heals wounds, and fulfills God's purpose for our lives.

FURTHER READING:

John 13:34-35; 1 Corinthians 13:4-7

PRAYER

Lord, thank You for the love You've poured into my heart through Christ. Teach me to love others selflessly and fulfill Your law through my actions. Amen.

CHALLENGE

Identify one relationship where you can practice selfless love this week. Take a specific step to show kindness, forgiveness, or encouragement.

DAY 5: LOVE FULFILLS THE LAW

Scripture Reading: Romans 13:9-10
Focus Verse: "The commandments… are summed
up in this one command: 'Love your neighbor as
yourself.' Love does no harm to a neighbor. Therefore, love is the fulfillment of the law."

DEVOTION

At the heart of God's law is love. Romans 13:9-10 emphasizes that every command—whether about honoring parents, avoiding theft, or rejecting envy—can be fulfilled through the single command to love our neighbor as ourselves. Love is not just an action but the motivation behind every action that honors God.

When we love others as God calls us to, we naturally avoid doing harm. Love prioritizes kindness over cruelty, honesty over deceit, and generosity over greed. This type of love requires humility and a heart transformed by God's grace.

Consider Paul, a business owner, who discovered that a rival company was spreading false rumors about his services. Though he was tempted to retaliate, he remembered Romans 13:10 and chose a different path. Instead of responding with anger, Paul focused on serving his customers with integrity and kindness. His actions reflected God's love, and over time, the rumors lost their power.

Loving others doesn't always come naturally, especially when we face opposition or hurt. But when we reflect on Christ's love for us—how He fulfilled the law through His sacrifice—we're empowered to love even in challenging circumstances.

Love fulfills the law because it aligns our hearts with God's purposes. It transforms relationships, strengthens communities, and points others to the One who is love.

FURTHER READING:

Galatians 5:14; Matthew 22:37-40

PRAYER

Father, thank You for showing me what true love looks like through Christ. Help me to love others as You have loved me, fulfilling Your law through my words and actions. Amen.

CHALLENGE

Think of one way you can demonstrate God's love to your "neighbor" today, whether it's a kind word, an act of service, or choosing forgiveness.

DAY 6: THE DAY IS NEAR

Scripture Reading: Romans 13:11-12
Focus Verse: "The hour has already come for you
to wake up from your slumber, because our salvation is nearer now than when we first believed. The
night is nearly over; the day is almost here."

DEVOTION

Time is short, and Paul's words in Romans 13:11-12 remind us to
live with urgency and purpose. The "day" he speaks of refers to Christ's
return—a day when the fullness of our salvation will be revealed. This
truth calls us to wake up, shed complacency, and live as children of light.

It's easy to fall into spiritual slumber, distracted by the busyness of life
or lulled into complacency by routine. But Paul urges us to recognize the
signs of the times and live with an eternal perspective. Every moment is an
opportunity to glorify God, share the gospel, and grow in Christlikeness.

Consider Anna, who realized she had been putting off sharing her
faith with a close friend. Romans 13:11 convicted her to stop waiting.
She prayed for courage and began having intentional conversations about
Christ. To her joy, her friend eventually came to know the Lord.

Living in light of Christ's return doesn't mean abandoning daily
responsibilities; it means approaching them with a kingdom mindset.
Whether through acts of kindness, faithful service, or sharing the hope of
salvation, every action can point others to the coming King.

The night of sin and brokenness is fading, and the dawn of Christ's
reign is near. Let this truth inspire you to live fully awake, walking in the
light of His promises.

FURTHER READING:

1 Thessalonians 5:4-6; Hebrews 10:24-25

PRAYER

Lord, wake me from spiritual complacency. Help me to live with urgency and purpose, reflecting Your light in all that I do. Teach me to use my time for Your glory. Amen.

CHALLENGE

Evaluate your daily routines. Identify one area where you can live more intentionally for Christ, whether in prayer, service, or sharing the gospel.

DAY 7: LET US BEHAVE PROPERLY

Scripture Reading: Romans 13:13-14
Focus Verse: "Let us behave properly as in the day, not in
sexual promiscutiy and sensuality, not in strife and jealousy."

DEVOTION:

In Romans 13, Paul calls us to live in a manner that reflects our
transformation in Christ. Today's verse, Romans 13:13, offers a clear
mandate: behave properly, as one would in the light of day. This imagery of daylight serves as a reminder that our lives should be transparent,
honest, and marked by integrity. When the world is cloaked in darkness,
hidden deeds thrive. In contrast, the brightness of day symbolizes truth
and accountability, challenging us to conduct ourselves in ways that hon-
or God and reflect His character.

This passage warns against lifestyles that obscure our true identity.
Paul lists behaviors like drunkenness, sexual immorality, and strife as
practices that belong to a time of moral darkness, not to those who have
embraced the light of Christ. As believers, our conduct should be so evident that it dispels any shadow of doubt regarding our commitment to
God's commandments. Living as children of the light means choosing
purity, self-control, and harmony over indulgence and discord.

Moreover, Paul's instructions encourage us to be role models in our
communities. When we consistently choose righteousness over vice, we
become beacons of hope and examples of God's transformative power.
Our behavior is not just a personal matter; it serves as a testimony to
others, inviting them to discover the freedom and joy found in living
according to God's will.

Embracing the call to behave properly is a daily challenge. It means
making choices that favor spiritual growth over momentary pleasure,
unity over conflict, and truth over deceit. As we navigate the complexities
of modern life, let the light of Christ guide us in every decision, ensuring

that our actions consistently shine with the brilliance of His love and righteousness.

FURTHER READING:
Ephesians 5:8-10; 1 Thessalonians 5:4-8

PRAYER:
Lord, help me to walk in Your light each day. Purify my thoughts and actions so that my life may reflect Your truth and love. Strengthen me to reject the temptations of darkness and embrace the path of righteousness. In Jesus' name, Amen.

CHALLENGE:
This week, evaluate one area of your life where darkness might still linger. Ask God for guidance to replace it with behaviors that truly reflect the light of Christ.

WALKING FURTHER:
WEEK 16 QUESTIONS

1. What does it mean to submit to authority, and how can you practice this in your daily life?

2. How does seeing authority as part of God's order change your view of it?

3. What are ways you can "pay" the debt of love to those around you?

4. Reflect on how love fulfills God's commands. How can you live this out in specific relationships?

5. Why does Paul call us to "wake up"? How can you live with greater spiritual urgency?

6. In what areas of your life can you more fully live as a testimony of God's love and light?

WEEK 17: UNDERSTANDING CHRISTIAN FREEDOM
(ROMANS 14)

ACCEPTING ONE ANOTHER
- ROMANS 14:1-2

HONOR GOD IN YOUR CONVICTIONS
- ROMANS 14:5-6

WE WILL ALL STAND BEFORE GOD
- ROMANS 14:10-12

DO NOT BE A STUMBLING BLOCK
- ROMANS 14:13

NOTHING IS UNCLEAN IN ITSELF
- ROMANS 14:14-16

PURSUING PEACE
- ROMANS 14:17-19

BUILDING UP, NOT TEARING DOWN
- ROMANS 14:20-23

DAY 1: ACCEPTING ONE ANOTHER

Scripture Reading: Romans 14:1-2
Focus Verse: "Accept the one whose faith is weak,
without quarreling over disputable matters."

DEVOTION

The early church was diverse, filled with believers from different backgrounds, convictions, and traditions. In Romans 14:1-2, Paul urges believers to accept one another, especially those whose faith may be weaker. Rather than quarrel over minor differences, Paul calls us to unity in Christ.

Accepting one another doesn't mean we must agree on every issue. It means choosing love and grace over judgment and criticism. Disputable matters—such as food, drink, or traditions—shouldn't divide the body of Christ. Instead, we are called to focus on what unites us: our shared faith in Jesus.

Consider Maria, who joined a small group where people held differing views on how to observe the Sabbath. Initially, she felt tempted to argue her point, but after meditating on Romans 14:1, she realized that her focus should be on loving her fellow believers rather than proving herself right. By prioritizing unity over personal preference, Maria helped foster a spirit of acceptance within the group.

When we accept one another, we reflect God's acceptance of us. He didn't wait for us to be perfect before extending His love; He embraced us while we were still sinners. By following His example, we create a community where people feel valued and supported in their spiritual growth.

FURTHER READING:

Colossians 3:13; Ephesians 4:2-3

PRAYER

Lord, teach me to accept others with grace and love. Help me to focus on unity in Christ rather than on differences that divide. Show me how to reflect Your heart in my relationships. Amen.

CHALLENGE

Think of someone in your church or community who has a different perspective from you. Take a step this week to connect with them, focusing on what unites you rather than what divides.

DAY 2: HONOR GOD IN YOUR CONVICTIONS

Scripture Reading: Romans 14:5-6
Focus Verse: "Each of them should be fully convinced in their own mind. Whoever regards one day as special does so to the Lord. Whoever eats meat does so to the Lord, for they give thanks to God."

DEVOTION

God calls us to live according to our convictions, not as a matter of pride but as an act of worship. In Romans 14:5-6, Paul addresses believers with differing practices, such as observing specific days or dietary choices. Instead of focusing on the differences, Paul emphasizes that these actions should honor God.

Our convictions should flow from a heart that seeks to glorify the Lord. Whether it's how we spend our time, handle resources, or make lifestyle choices, our goal should always be to please God. When we act in faith, trusting Him to guide us, our lives become an offering of thanksgiving.

Paul's teaching reminds us to avoid imposing our convictions on others or judging their decisions. What matters is that each person acts with sincerity and reverence toward God. This attitude fosters unity and mutual respect within the body of Christ.

Consider Josh and Kevin, who held opposing views on how to celebrate holidays. Josh preferred traditional celebrations, while Kevin enjoyed exploring new ways to honor God during those times. Instead of arguing, they chose to respect each other's convictions, recognizing that their shared goal was to glorify the Lord. Their friendship grew as they focused on their common faith rather than their differences.

Living by conviction requires humility and dependence on God. It's not about proving we're right but about seeking His will in every decision. When we honor Him in our convictions, we encourage others to do the same.

FURTHER READING:
1 Corinthians 10:31; Galatians 5:13

PRAYER
Lord, help me to live by convictions that honor You. Teach me to respect others' choices and to seek Your glory in everything I do. Amen.

CHALLENGE
Evaluate one of your personal convictions this week. Ask God to confirm that it aligns with His Word and commit to living it out as an act of worship.

DAY 3: WE WILL ALL STAND BEFORE GOD

Scripture Reading: Romans 14:10-12
Focus Verse: "For we will all stand before God's judgment seat. It is written: 'As surely as I live,' says the Lord, 'every knee will bow before me; every tongue will acknowledge God.'"

DEVOTION

One day, every person will stand before God's judgment seat. Romans 14:10-12 reminds us that God alone is the righteous Judge. This truth shifts our focus from judging others to examining our own hearts and lives.

Paul's message is clear: stop judging fellow believers over disputable matters. Instead, remember that we are all accountable to God. When we focus on our relationship with Him, we grow in humility and grace toward others. Knowing that God is the ultimate Judge frees us from the burden of trying to control or criticize others' choices.

Consider Lisa, who often felt frustrated by how her friends managed their time and priorities. She judged them silently, thinking they should be more like her. After reading Romans 14:10, Lisa realized she was focusing on others' shortcomings instead of her own walk with Christ. She began praying for her friends and asking God to help her trust Him as the Judge.

Standing before God's judgment seat isn't something to fear if we are in Christ. His grace covers our sins, and His Spirit empowers us to live in obedience. But this accountability should inspire us to take our faith seriously, striving to honor Him in all we do.

When we acknowledge God as the righteous Judge, we are reminded of His sovereignty and justice. This perspective encourages us to live faithfully, love generously, and trust Him to guide others according to His will.

FURTHER READING:
2 Corinthians 5:10; Philippians 2:10-11

PRAYER
Lord, thank You for being the righteous Judge. Help me to trust Your justice and focus on my own walk with You instead of judging others. Teach me to live in a way that honors You. Amen.

CHALLENGE
Reflect on a situation where you've been tempted to judge someone else. Surrender it to God, trusting Him as the ultimate Judge.

DAY 4: DO NOT BE A STUMBLING BLOCK

Scripture Reading: Romans 14:13
Focus Verse: "Therefore let us stop passing judgment on one another. Instead, make up your mind not to put any stumbling block or obstacle in the way of a brother or sister."

DEVOTION

As Christians, we are called to build each other up, not tear each other down. Romans 14:13 reminds us of the responsibility we have to ensure our actions don't cause others to stumble in their faith. This means being mindful of how our choices and behavior impact those around us.

A stumbling block can take many forms—criticism, selfishness, or even freedom taken too far. While we are free in Christ, Paul urges us to prioritize love over liberty. If something we do offends or confuses another believer, it's worth considering whether our actions honor God and strengthen His body.

Beth loved her weekly Bible study group but noticed a newer member, Sarah, seemed uncomfortable with the group's social traditions. Beth approached Sarah with compassion, asking how she could help her feel more at ease. By listening and adjusting some activities, Beth removed obstacles that could have hindered Sarah's faith journey.

Avoiding stumbling blocks doesn't mean abandoning your convictions. Instead, it's about walking in love, putting others' spiritual growth above personal preferences. This reflects the humility and grace of Christ, who came not to please Himself but to serve others.

When we live with this mindset, we create an environment where faith can flourish. Removing stumbling blocks fosters unity, builds trust, and points others to the love of Jesus.

FURTHER READING:

1 Corinthians 8:9-13; Galatians 5:13

PRAYER

Lord, help me to live in a way that builds up others. Show me where my actions might create stumbling blocks, and teach me to walk in love and humility. Amen.

CHALLENGE

Identify one area in your life where your actions might unintentionally create a stumbling block for others. Make an intentional change to prioritize their spiritual growth.

DAY 5: NOTHING IS UNCLEAN IN ITSELF

Scripture Reading: Romans 14:14-16

Focus Verse: "I am convinced, being fully persuaded in the Lord Jesus, that nothing is unclean in itself. But if anyone regards something as unclean, then for that person it is unclean."

DEVOTION

Paul addresses a sensitive issue in Romans 14:14-16: the tension between personal freedom in Christ and the consciences of fellow believers. While nothing is inherently unclean, Paul teaches that we should be mindful of how our actions affect others. Loving others means valuing their spiritual well-being over our personal liberty.

Freedom in Christ is a gift. It liberates us from legalism and allows us to enjoy God's blessings. However, freedom should never come at the expense of another person's faith. If something we consider acceptable causes a brother or sister to stumble, love compels us to reconsider our choices.

David enjoyed eating certain foods that his new Christian friend, Peter, believed were wrong due to his cultural background. Instead of asserting his freedom, David chose to avoid those foods when dining with Peter, demonstrating respect for his conscience. Over time, Peter grew in his understanding of Christian liberty, but David's love and sensitivity helped preserve their unity.

Paul's message reminds us that relationships matter more than rights. While we are free to enjoy the good things God has given us, love requires us to prioritize others' spiritual health. This doesn't mean living in fear of offending others but being intentional about how our choices align with God's call to love.

When we put love into action, we create an atmosphere where others can grow in faith without unnecessary obstacles.

FURTHER READING:
1 Corinthians 10:23-24; Galatians 5:13

PRAYER
Lord, thank You for the freedom I have in Christ. Help me to use that freedom wisely, always seeking to build up others and honor You in all I do. Amen.

CHALLENGE
Reflect on an area where your actions could affect the conscience of another believer. Ask God for wisdom in how to lovingly navigate that situation.

DAY 6: PURSUING PEACE

Scripture Reading: Romans 14:17-19
Focus Verse: *"Let us therefore make every effort to do what leads to peace and to mutual edification."*

DEVOTION

Peace is not just the absence of conflict but the presence of harmony within the body of Christ. In Romans 14:17-19, Paul calls believers to pursue peace and work toward building one another up. This requires intentionality, humility, and a heart focused on God's kingdom.

The pursuit of peace begins with understanding what matters most. Paul reminds us that the kingdom of God is not about external rules or disputes but about righteousness, peace, and joy in the Holy Spirit. When we focus on these priorities, we foster an environment where relationships can thrive.

Maria found herself caught in a heated debate at church about worship styles. Instead of fueling the argument, she gently reminded the group that their shared love for Christ mattered more than their personal preferences. Her willingness to focus on unity helped the group refocus on their mission and strengthened their bond.

Pursuing peace doesn't mean avoiding hard conversations or pretending disagreements don't exist. It means approaching conflicts with grace and a desire for resolution rather than division. It means choosing words and actions that encourage rather than tear down.

When we pursue peace, we reflect the character of Christ, who came to reconcile us to God and to one another. This witness of unity and love strengthens the church and points a watching world to the Prince of Peace.

FURTHER READING:

Matthew 5:9; Ephesians 4:3

PRAYER

Father, help me to pursue peace in my relationships. Teach me to prioritize unity and to encourage others in their faith. Let my actions reflect the harmony of Your kingdom. Amen.

CHALLENGE

Identify one area where conflict or division has crept into your relationships. Take a specific step this week to pursue peace, whether through a conversation, forgiveness, or prayer.

DAY 7: BUILDING UP, NOT TEARING DOWN

Scripture Reading: Romans 14:20-23

Focus Verse: "Do not destroy the work of God for the sake of food. All food is clean, but it is wrong for a person to eat anything that causes someone else to stumble."

DEVOTION

The work of God in someone's life is precious, and Paul's words in Romans 14:20-23 remind us to protect that work with love and care. While we may enjoy freedom in Christ, our choices should never hinder another believer's spiritual growth. Instead, we are called to build each other up in faith.

Paul highlights the potential harm of prioritizing personal liberty over love. While something may be permissible for us, it can create confusion or conflict for others who view it differently. True Christian maturity seeks the good of others, even at the cost of personal preferences.

Consider Clara, who enjoyed attending events that her friend Mary found spiritually troubling. Rather than insisting on her freedom, Clara chose to avoid those activities when spending time with Mary. Her decision showed respect for Mary's conscience and strengthened their bond as sisters in Christ.

Building others up requires sensitivity and a commitment to unity. It means listening to their concerns, understanding their perspective, and adjusting our actions when needed. This reflects Christ's humility, who laid down His rights to serve and save us.

When we prioritize love over liberty, we create an atmosphere of encouragement and trust. This not only strengthens individual faith but also glorifies God, showing the world what it means to live as His people.

FURTHER READING:

1 Corinthians 10:32-33; Galatians 6:2

PRAYER

Lord, teach me to build others up in faith. Help me to prioritize love and unity over personal freedom, reflecting Your humility and grace. Amen.

CHALLENGE

Think of one way your actions could unintentionally hinder someone's faith. Take a step to adjust or address that action this week, prioritizing their spiritual growth.

WALKING FURTHER:
WEEK 17 QUESTIONS

1. How can you practice acceptance of others' differences in your daily life?

2. What does it mean to honor God in your convictions?

3. Reflect on the reality that we will each stand before God. How does this influence your interactions with others?

4. Why is it important not to be a stumbling block to others?

5. How can you pursue peace within your relationships?

6. In what ways can you build others up instead of tearing them down?

7. How does respect for others' convictions strengthen unity in the body of Christ?

WEEK 18: BEARING WITH ONE ANOTHER IN LOVE AND UNITY (ROMANS 15:1-13)

BEARING THE WEAKNESSES OF OTHERS
   – ROMANS 15:1

BUILDING EACH OTHER UP
   – ROMANS 15:2

CHRIST AS OUR EXAMPLE
   – ROMANS 15:3-4

UNITY THROUGH PATIENCE AND ENCOURAGEMENT
   –ROMANS 15:5-6

GLORIFYING GOD TOGETHER
   – ROMANS 15:6

ACCEPT ONE ANOTHER
   – ROMANS 15:7

HOPE AND JOY IN BELIEVING
   – ROMANS 15:13

DAY 1: BEARING THE WEAKNESSES OF OTHERS

Scripture Reading: Romans 15:1
Focus Verse: "We who are strong ought to bear with the failings of the weak and not to please ourselves."

DEVOTION

Paul's call in Romans 15:1 challenges us to carry the burdens of others rather than focus solely on our own comfort. Strength in the Christian life is not a privilege to boast about but a responsibility to serve. Those who are spiritually mature are called to support and encourage those who may be struggling in their faith.

Bearing with the weaknesses of others requires humility and selflessness. It means choosing patience over frustration and grace over judgment. Instead of criticizing someone's shortcomings, we are called to walk alongside them, helping them grow in their relationship with Christ.

Sarah, a Bible study leader, noticed that a new member, Ellie, struggled to understand the material. Instead of feeling annoyed, Sarah took extra time to explain concepts to Ellie, encouraging her to ask questions. Over time, Ellie's confidence and understanding grew, thanks to Sarah's willingness to bear her weaknesses.

This kind of love reflects the heart of Jesus. He bore the ultimate burden of our sin on the cross, showing us what true selflessness looks like. When we bear the weaknesses of others, we imitate His example and create a community of grace and support.

Bearing with one another doesn't mean ignoring sin or enabling harmful behavior. It means lovingly helping others in their struggles while pointing them to Christ, who is the source of true strength.

FURTHER READING:

Galatians 6:2; Colossians 3:13

PRAYER

Lord, thank You for bearing my burdens and weaknesses. Teach me to extend the same grace to others, helping them grow in their faith and reflecting Your love. Amen.

CHALLENGE

Identify someone in your life who is struggling spiritually or emotionally. Find a way to support and encourage them this week, bearing their burden with patience and love.

DAY 2: BUILDING EACH OTHER UP

Scripture Reading: Romans 15:2
Focus Verse: "Each of us should please our neigh-
bors for their good, to build them up."

DEVOTION

The Christian life is not about self-interest; it's about serving others
and building them up in faith. Romans 15:2 reminds us that our words
and actions should encourage and strengthen those around us, helping
them grow closer to God.

Building each other up requires intentionality. It means seeking
the good of others, offering encouragement, and using our gifts to bless
them. This isn't about flattering others or meeting selfish motives but
genuinely desiring their spiritual and emotional well-being.

Consider John, who noticed a coworker struggling with discour-
agement. Instead of offering empty platitudes, John prayed for wisdom
and shared a Scripture verse that had encouraged him in his own trials.
His words brought comfort and hope, showing his coworker the love of
Christ in a tangible way.

The Bible reminds us that our words have the power to build up or
tear down (Proverbs 18:21). When we choose to speak life, we reflect
God's character and create an atmosphere of grace and encouragement.
Even small acts of kindness can have a profound impact on someone's
faith journey.

As believers, we are part of one body, called to edify and support
one another. When we focus on building others up, we glorify God and
strengthen His church, creating a community that reflects His love.

FURTHER READING:

1 Thessalonians 5:11; Ephesians 4:29

PRAYER

Lord, teach me to use my words and actions to build others up. Help me to seek their good and encourage them in their walk with You. Show me how to reflect Your love in all I do. Amen.

CHALLENGE

Look for an opportunity to build someone up this week. Whether through a kind word, a thoughtful gesture, or an act of service, be intentional about encouraging their faith.

DAY 3: CHRIST AS OUR EXAMPLE

Scripture Reading: Romans 15:3-4
Focus Verse: "For even Christ did not please Himself but, as it is written: 'The insults of those who insult you have fallen on me.'"

DEVOTION

Jesus is the ultimate example of selflessness and humility. In Romans 15:3-4, Paul points us to Christ, who bore the insults and burdens of others for the sake of God's glory. His life teaches us what it means to live for others rather than ourselves.

Jesus didn't seek His own comfort or popularity. He endured rejection, suffering, and death so that we could experience salvation. His selflessness reminds us that the Christian life isn't about pleasing ourselves but about glorifying God and serving others with love and grace.

Consider Emily, who volunteered to lead her church's youth group despite her busy schedule. When things became challenging, she wanted to step back, but as she meditated on Romans 15:3, she found strength in Christ's example. She realized that her service wasn't about her convenience but about pointing young people to Jesus.

Paul also emphasizes the importance of Scripture in shaping our attitudes and actions. Through God's word, we find encouragement and hope, equipping us to follow Christ's example in our daily lives.

When we live like Christ, putting others first and bearing their burdens, we reflect His love to a world in need. This kind of selflessness requires humility, reliance on God, and a willingness to sacrifice our own desires for His greater purpose.

FURTHER READING:

Philippians 2:5-8; John 13:14-15

PRAYER

Lord, thank You for the example of Christ. Teach me to live with humility and selflessness, putting others before myself. Help me to glorify You in my words and actions. Amen.

CHALLENGE

Identify one area where you can follow Christ's example of selflessness. Take a specific step this week to serve someone in need, even if it's inconvenient.

DAY 4: UNITY THROUGH PATIENCE AND ENCOURAGEMENT

Scripture Reading: Romans 15:5-6

Focus Verse: "May the God who gives endurance and encouragement give you the same attitude of mind toward each other that Christ Jesus had, so that with one mind and one voice you may glorify the God and Father of our Lord Jesus Christ."

DEVOTION

Unity among believers is a powerful testimony to the world. In Romans 15:5-6, Paul reminds us that unity is possible when we follow Christ's example of patience and encouragement. By seeking harmony with one another, we bring glory to God.

Unity doesn't mean uniformity. It's not about everyone looking or thinking the same but about having the same attitude of love, humility, and service that Christ demonstrated. This requires endurance to bear with one another's weaknesses and encouragement to uplift each other in faith.

Alex and Jordan, members of a worship team, often clashed over musical styles. Their disagreements sometimes distracted from their ministry. After reading Romans 15:5, they decided to pray together before every rehearsal, asking God for unity. Over time, their shared focus on glorifying God replaced their personal preferences, strengthening their relationship and ministry.

Patience is key to maintaining unity. It allows us to navigate differences without frustration or division. Encouragement helps us see the best in others and build them up, fostering an environment of grace and support.

When believers are united, their collective voice glorifies God and draws others to Him. This kind of unity reflects the love and humility of Christ, showing the world the transformative power of His Spirit.

FURTHER READING:
Colossians 3:13-14; Ephesians 4:2-3

PRAYER
Lord, help me to seek unity with my brothers and sisters in Christ. Teach me patience and give me a heart that encourages others. Let our unity bring glory to Your name. Amen.

CHALLENGE
Reflect on a relationship where unity has been difficult to maintain. Pray for patience and encouragement, and take a step this week to restore harmony.

DAY 5: GLORIFYING GOD TOGETHER

Scripture Reading: Romans 15:6
Focus Verse: "So that with one mind and one voice you may glorify the God and Father of our Lord Jesus Christ."

DEVOTION

Worship is at its most powerful when believers glorify God together, united in heart and purpose. Romans 15:6 paints a beautiful picture of the church as a community that speaks and sings with one voice, offering praise to God in harmony.

This unity doesn't come from human effort alone. It flows from the work of the Holy Spirit, who enables us to lay aside our differences and focus on what truly matters: glorifying God. When we unite in worship, we demonstrate the beauty of God's kingdom to the world.

Consider Rebecca's small church, which was filled with people from diverse cultural and social backgrounds. Initially, differences caused misunderstandings and tension. But as they prioritized prayer and worship together, their focus shifted from their individual preferences to their shared faith in Christ. Over time, their unity became a testimony of God's glory to their community.

Glorifying God together isn't limited to singing hymns or attending services. It's reflected in how we live, work, and serve alongside one another with love and humility. When we live in unity, our collective witness points others to Christ, showing them the transforming power of His grace.

This shared worship glorifies God and strengthens the body of Christ. It reminds us that we are part of something greater than ourselves—a global church that exists to exalt the Lord and proclaim His glory.

FURTHER READING:
Psalm 34:3; John 17:20-23

PRAYER
Father, thank You for the gift of unity in worship. Teach me to glorify You alongside my brothers and sisters in Christ, reflecting Your love to the world. Let our shared voice bring You honor. Amen.

CHALLENGE
This week, invite someone to join you in worship, whether at church, in prayer, or in service. Together, glorify God with one heart and one voice.

DAY 6: ACCEPT ONE ANOTHER

Scripture Reading: Romans 15:7
Focus Verse: "Accept one another, then, just as Christ
accepted you, in order to bring praise to God."

DEVOTION

Acceptance is at the heart of Christian community. Romans 15:7 calls us to embrace one another, not based on merit or similarity, but as Christ has accepted us—with grace, love, and humility. When we do this, we glorify God and reflect His welcoming nature to the world.

Jesus didn't wait for us to clean up our lives before accepting us. He met us in our brokenness, offering forgiveness and restoration. Similarly, our acceptance of others should be unconditional, rooted in the understanding that we are all recipients of God's grace.

Consider Mark and Tim, two members of a men's group who struggled to connect due to their differing personalities. Mark, a reserved and analytical thinker, found Tim's outgoing and emotional approach overwhelming at times. But as they meditated on Romans 15:7 together, they learned to value their differences as strengths, appreciating how God had uniquely shaped them to grow and serve together.

Accepting one another doesn't mean ignoring sin or compromising truth. Instead, it means creating a space where people feel loved and valued as they seek to grow in their faith. Acceptance fosters unity and reflects the heart of God, who welcomes all who come to Him through Christ.

When we accept others, we testify to the power of the gospel, showing that God's love transcends differences and transforms lives. This kind of community brings praise to God and draws others to Him.

FURTHER READING:

Colossians 3:12-13; John 6:37

PRAYER

Lord, thank You for accepting me as I am and transforming me by Your grace. Teach me to accept others with the same love and humility, bringing glory to Your name. Amen.

CHALLENGE

Identify someone you've struggled to accept fully. Reach out to them this week with an act of kindness or encouragement, reflecting Christ's love.

DAY 7: HOPE AND JOY IN BELIEVING

Scripture Reading: Romans 15:13
Focus Verse: "May the God of hope fill you with all joy
and peace as you trust in him, so that you may overflow with hope by the power of the Holy Spirit."

DEVOTION

Hope is a gift that transforms our hearts and minds, filling us with
joy and peace as we trust in God. In Romans 15:13, Paul reminds us
that this hope is not dependent on circumstances but is sustained by the
power of the Holy Spirit. It is a hope that overflows, touching every part
of our lives and spilling into the lives of others.

True hope comes from trusting in God's promises. When we focus
on His faithfulness, we experience a peace that calms our fears and a joy
that lifts our spirits, even in the midst of trials. This hope is not wishful
thinking but a confident assurance that God is in control and working
for our good.

Samantha faced a season of uncertainty after losing her job. As she
meditated on Romans 15:13, she began to pray daily, asking God to fill
her with His hope. Slowly, her fear gave way to trust, and her joy re-
turned as she remembered God's past faithfulness. She even found herself
encouraging others who were struggling, sharing the overflow of hope
she had received.

The power of the Holy Spirit is key to living in this hope. We cannot
manufacture it on our own, but as we abide in Christ and rely on His
Spirit, hope becomes an anchor for our souls. This hope not only sustains
us but also draws others to the God of hope.

FURTHER READING:

Hebrews 6:19; Philippians 4:7

PRAYER

Lord, thank You for being the God of hope. Fill me with Your joy and peace as I trust in You. Let my life overflow with hope, pointing others to Your faithfulness. Amen.

CHALLENGE

Write down a specific area where you need to trust God more fully. Pray daily this week, asking the Holy Spirit to fill you with hope, joy, and peace in that situation.

WALKING FURTHER:
WEEK 18 QUESTIONS

1. How can you bear others' weaknesses with patience?

2. What does building each other up look like in your life?

3. How does following Christ's example challenge you to serve selflessly?

4. What steps can you take to promote unity in your relationships?

5. Why is worshiping God together important for unity?

6. How can you accept others as Christ has accepted you?

7. What areas of your life need God's joy and peace in believing?

WEEK 19: PAUL'S CLOSING WORDS AND MINISTRY PARTNERSHIPS
(ROMANS 15:14-16:27)

FILLED WITH KNOWLEDGE AND ABLE TO INSTRUCT
 – ROMANS 15:14

BOLD IN REMINDING
 – ROMANS 15:15-16

MINISTERING THE GOSPEL
 – ROMANS 15:17-19

AIMING WHERE CHRIST HAS NOT BEEN NAMED
 – ROMANS 15:20-21

PARTNERS IN MINISTRY
 – ROMANS 15:22-24

SERVING THE SAINTS
 – ROMANS 15:25-27

STRIVING TOGETHER IN PRAYER
 – ROMANS 15:30-33

DAY 1: FILLED WITH KNOWLEDGE AND ABLE TO INSTRUCT

Scripture Reading: Romans 15:14

Focus Verse: "I myself am convinced, my brothers and sisters, that you yourselves are full of goodness, filled with knowledge and competent to instruct one another."

DEVOTION

Paul's words in Romans 15:14 are a reminder that every believer has a role in teaching and encouraging others in their faith. The ability to instruct isn't limited to pastors or scholars; it's a responsibility shared by all who are growing in the knowledge of God.

Paul commends the Roman believers for being "full of goodness" and "filled with knowledge." These qualities reflect a life transformed by the Holy Spirit and grounded in Scripture. When we immerse ourselves in God's word, we gain the wisdom needed to guide and encourage others, building up the body of Christ.

Consider Leah, a young woman who had recently joined her church's discipleship group. Though she didn't see herself as a teacher, her consistent study of Scripture allowed her to share insights that encouraged her group. Her willingness to instruct others from a heart of humility and goodness made a lasting impact.

Being competent to instruct one another doesn't mean having all the answers. It means being willing to share what God has taught us, whether through His Word, prayer, or personal experience. Our goal is not to elevate ourselves but to glorify God and build up others in love.

As we grow in goodness and knowledge, we become better equipped to encourage, teach, and challenge one another, fulfilling God's call to make disciples and strengthen His church.

FURTHER READING:
2 Timothy 3:16-17; Colossians 3:16

PRAYER
Lord, thank You for the knowledge and wisdom found in Your Word. Help me to grow in goodness and to use what I've learned to encourage and instruct others. Amen.

CHALLENGE
Identify someone in your life who could benefit from encouragement or instruction. Share a Scripture or lesson with them this week to help them grow in their faith.

DAY 2: BOLD IN REMINDING

Scripture Reading: Romans 15:15-16
Focus Verse: "Yet I have written you quite boldly on some points to remind you of them again, because of the grace God gave me to be a minister of Christ Jesus to the Gentiles."

DEVOTION

Sometimes, we need bold reminders of the truths we already know. In Romans 15:15-16, Paul acknowledges that his words may seem direct, but they are written out of love and a sense of divine calling. He reminds the Roman believers of their identity and mission in Christ, urging them to remain faithful.

Boldness in reminding others is not about criticism but about love. Paul wasn't writing to condemn but to encourage and strengthen the church. His boldness came from his awareness of God's grace and his responsibility as a minister of the gospel.

Sarah, a mentor to young adults in her church, often hesitated to challenge her mentees when they strayed from biblical principles. After reading Romans 15:15, she realized that boldness in speaking the truth was a vital part of her role. With humility and love, she began reminding her mentees of God's truth, helping them grow in their faith.

Being bold in reminding others requires humility and wisdom. It's about speaking the truth in love, motivated by a desire to see others flourish in their walk with Christ. Just as Paul relied on God's grace to fulfill his ministry, we, too, can trust the Holy Spirit to guide us in encouraging and challenging others.

When we remind one another of God's word, we strengthen the church and help each other stay rooted in faith. These reminders are not burdensome but life-giving, drawing us closer to God and His purposes.

FURTHER READING:
2 Peter 1:12-13; Ephesians 4:15

PRAYER
Lord, thank You for the boldness of Your Word. Help me to remind others of Your truth with humility and love. Give me courage to speak boldly when needed, always pointing others to You. Amen.

CHALLENGE
This week, identify someone who might need a loving reminder of God's truth. Reach out to them with encouragement, pointing them back to Scripture.

DAY 3: MINISTERING THE GOSPEL

Scripture Reading: Romans 15:17-19

Focus Verse: "Therefore I glory in Christ Jesus in my service to God. I will not venture to speak of anything except what Christ has accomplished through me in leading the Gentiles to obey God by what I have said and done."

DEVOTION

Paul's ministry was centered on the gospel of Christ. In Romans 15:17-19, he takes no credit for his accomplishments but gives glory to God for working through him to bring salvation to the Gentiles. His words remind us that ministering the gospel is not about personal achievement but about pointing others to Christ.

The gospel is powerful because it is God's work, not ours. Paul's ministry succeeded because it was empowered by the Holy Spirit, not by human effort. His focus was on what Christ accomplished through him, a model for all believers to follow.

Consider Nathan, a high school teacher who often prayed for opportunities to share the gospel with his students. One day, a student asked him how he handled stress with such peace. Nathan shared his faith in Christ, leading to a life-changing conversation. Later, Nathan reflected on how it was God who created the moment and gave him the words to speak.

Ministering the gospel involves both words and actions. Paul's life showed that the way we live is just as important as what we say. When our actions align with the gospel, they amplify our testimony and draw others to Christ.

We are all called to minister the gospel, whether in our workplaces, communities, or homes. As we rely on the Holy Spirit, God works through us to bring others to Him, transforming lives for His glory.

FURTHER READING:

1 Corinthians 2:4-5; Matthew 28:19-20

PRAYER

Lord, thank You for the privilege of sharing the gospel. Help me to rely on Your Spirit and to glorify You in all that I say and do. Use me as Your instrument to lead others to Christ. Amen.

CHALLENGE

Look for an opportunity this week to minister the gospel through your words or actions. Pray for God's guidance and be ready to share His love

DAY 4: AIMING WHERE CHRIST HAS NOT BEEN NAMED

Scripture Reading: Romans 15:20-21
Focus Verse: "It has always been my ambition to preach the gospel where Christ was not known, so that I would not be building on someone else's foundation."

DEVOTION

Paul's ambition to preach the gospel where Christ had not been named reflects his deep passion for fulfilling the Great Commission. In Romans 15:20-21, he shares his desire to reach those who had never heard of Jesus, quoting Isaiah to emphasize that God's plan includes all nations.

This mission required courage, perseverance, and a willingness to go beyond what was comfortable. Paul's heart for the unreached challenges us to think about how we can participate in spreading the gospel, whether through going, supporting, or praying.

Consider Sarah, who felt called to support missionaries serving in remote villages. Though she couldn't go herself, she began praying daily for an unreached people group and giving financially to their mission. Her contributions became part of God's work in bringing the gospel to those who had never heard it.

Sharing Christ with those who don't know Him is not limited to far-off places. It may mean reaching out to a neighbor, coworker, or friend who has yet to hear the good news. God calls each of us to have a heart for the lost, whether near or far.

When we aim to share Christ where He is not known, we align ourselves with God's global mission. Our willingness to step out in faith allows us to participate in His redemptive plan, bringing light to those who live in spiritual darkness.

FURTHER READING:

Matthew 24:14; Acts 13:47

PRAYER

Lord, give me a heart for the unreached. Show me how I can participate in sharing the gospel, whether through going, supporting, or praying. Use me to bring Your name to those who have never heard it. Amen.

CHALLENGE

Identify an individual or group in your life or community who may
not know Christ. Commit to praying for them and look for an opportunity to share the gospel with them.

DAY 5: PARTNERS IN MINISTRY

Scripture Reading: Romans 15:22-24
Focus Verse: "I plan to do so when I go to Spain. I hope to see you while passing through and to have you assist me on my journey there, after I have enjoyed your company for a while."

DEVOTION

Paul understood the value of partnerships in ministry. In Romans 15:22-24, he expresses his desire to visit the Roman church and receive their support for his mission to Spain. This passage highlights the collaborative nature of gospel work, showing that no one accomplishes God's mission alone.

Ministry partnerships involve mutual encouragement, prayer, and resources. Paul's willingness to ask for assistance reflects humility and a recognition that every believer plays a role in advancing God's kingdom. His focus wasn't on personal gain but on fulfilling God's calling with the help of the body of Christ.

Consider Jessica, who felt called to serve as a missionary overseas. She relied on her church family for prayer, financial support, and encouragement. While she worked in the field, her church supported her mission from home, strengthening her through their partnership. Together, they shared in the joy of seeing lives transformed by the gospel.

Partnerships in ministry remind us that we are part of a larger body, each with unique gifts and roles. Some are called to go, while others are called to send, but all are vital to God's mission. These relationships strengthen the church and create a network of support that glorifies God.

By partnering in ministry, we reflect the unity and purpose of the body of Christ. Whether through financial giving, prayer, or practical help, our contributions become part of God's redemptive work in the world.

FURTHER READING:

1 Corinthians 3:9; Philippians 1:3-5

PRAYER

Lord, thank You for the gift of ministry partnerships. Teach me to support others in their calling and to work together for Your glory. Help me to serve faithfully in the role You have given me. Amen.

CHALLENGE

Identify someone in ministry or missions whom you can support. Write them a note of encouragement, commit to praying for them, or offer practical assistance.

DAY 6: SERVING THE SAINTS

Scripture Reading: Romans 15:25-27
Focus Verse: "Now, however, I am on my way to Jerusalem in the service of the Lord's people there."

DEVOTION

Serving the saints is a tangible way to express God's love within the body of Christ. In Romans 15:25-27, Paul shares his plans to deliver a contribution to the believers in Jerusalem, collected from Gentile churches. This act of generosity reflects the interconnectedness of God's people and the call to serve one another in times of need.

Paul highlights the joy and responsibility of serving fellow believers. The Gentile churches recognized their spiritual debt to the Jewish believers who had shared the gospel with them. Their financial gift wasn't merely an obligation—it was an expression of gratitude and unity in Christ.

Consider Emily, a single mother in her congregation, who faced unexpected medical bills. Her church family came together to provide meals, financial support, and prayer. Their service not only met her physical needs but also strengthened her faith and sense of belonging in the church.

Serving the saints is about more than meeting material needs. It's about demonstrating the love and care of Christ, fostering unity within His body. Whether through financial giving, acts of service, or prayer, every believer has a role to play in supporting one another.

When we serve the saints, we glorify God and testify to the world about the transformative power of His love. Our acts of service strengthen the church and deepen our relationships with one another.

FURTHER READING:

Galatians 6:10; 1 Peter 4:10

PRAYER

Lord, thank You for the privilege of serving Your people. Teach me to recognize the needs of others and to respond with love and generosity. Help me to reflect Your care in all I do. Amen.

CHALLENGE

Look for an opportunity to serve a fellow believer this week. Whether through prayer, financial help, or a kind gesture, show the love of Christ in action.

DAY 7: STRIVING TOGETHER IN PRAYER

Scripture Reading: Romans 15:30-33
Focus Verse: "I urge you, brothers and sisters, by our
Lord Jesus Christ and by the love of the Spirit, to join
me in my struggle by praying to God for me."

DEVOTION

Paul understood the power of prayer and its role in ministry. In Romans 15:30-33, he appeals to the Roman believers to join him in striving together through prayer. This isn't a casual request—it's an urgent plea for partnership in the spiritual battle he faces.

Prayer is an essential part of ministry and the Christian life. When we pray for one another, we join in their struggles, standing together in faith. Paul's words remind us that prayer isn't a passive activity but an active form of spiritual warfare, fueled by the love of Christ and the Spirit.

Consider David, who supported his missionary friend, Sarah, through regular intercession. Though he couldn't join her in the field, his prayers strengthened her and provided divine guidance and protection. When Sarah faced challenges, she often felt peace, knowing her church family was praying for her.

Striving together in prayer unites believers across distances, creating a spiritual bond that transcends circumstances. It reminds us of our dependence on God and the privilege we have to intercede for one another.

When we pray for others, we align ourselves with God's will, trusting Him to work in ways beyond our understanding. Our prayers not only uplift those we intercede for but also deepen our faith and connection with the Lord.

FURTHER READING:

Colossians 4:2-3; James 5:16

PRAYER

Lord, thank You for the gift of prayer. Teach me to strive in prayer for others, joining in their struggles and trusting You to work in their lives. Help me to be faithful in lifting up my brothers and sisters in Christ. Amen.

CHALLENGE

This week, commit to praying daily for someone in ministry or facing a spiritual battle. Reach out to them and let them know you are interceding on their behalf.

WALKING FURTHER:
WEEK 19 QUESTIONS

1. How does Paul's reminder to instruct and encourage others apply to your life?

2. What area of your life can you be bold in reminding others of God's truth?

3. How can you share what Christ has done in your life to minister to others?

4. What does it mean to partner in ministry, and how can you support others?

5. How can you support the needs of the saints, both near and far?

6. Why is striving together in prayer powerful in ministry?

7. What steps can you take to make intercessory prayer a regular part of your life?

WEEK 20: ENCOURAGEMENT IN FELLOWSHIP
(ROMANS 16)

COMMENDING FAITHFUL SERVANTS
  – ROMANS 16:1-2

HONORING FELLOW WORKERS
  – ROMANS 16:3-4

RECOGNIZING HARD WORK
  – ROMANS 16:6

BROTHERS AND SISTERS IN CHRIST
  – ROMANS 16:7-10

WELCOMING ONE ANOTHER IN LOVE
  – ROMANS 16:11-13

UNITY AND VIGILANCE
  – ROMANS 16:17-18

GLORY TO GOD THROUGH CHRIST
  – ROMANS 16:25-27

DAY 1: COMMENDING FAITHFUL SERVANTS

Scripture Reading: Romans 16:1-2
Focus Verse: "I commend to you our sister Phoebe,
a deacon of the church in Cenchreae. I ask you to receive her in the Lord in a way worthy of His people and
to give her any help she may need from you, for she has
been the benefactor of many people, including me."

DEVOTION

Paul begins Romans 16 by commending Phoebe, a faithful servant of the church in Cenchreae. His words honor her role in ministry and encourage the believers in Rome to support her. This passage reminds us of the importance of recognizing and uplifting those who serve faithfully in the body of Christ.

Phoebe's life reflects the heart of servanthood. As a benefactor and deacon, she gave generously of her time, resources, and gifts to support God's work. Paul's commendation highlights the value of her contributions and sets an example for how we should honor and support those who serve.

Consider Emily, a quiet woman in her church who faithfully organizes meals for families in need. Though her work often goes unnoticed, her acts of service bring comfort and strength to many. When her pastor publicly thanked her during a church service, it encouraged Emily and inspired others to follow her example.

Honoring faithful servants is not about elevating individuals but about glorifying God through their obedience and sacrifice. It's an opportunity to express gratitude and foster a culture of encouragement within the church.

When we commend others, we remind them of their impact and inspire them to continue serving with joy. This practice strengthens the body of Christ and reflects the love and unity we are called to as His people.

FURTHER READING:
Hebrews 6:10; Philippians 2:3-4

PRAYER
Lord, thank You for the faithful servants in Your church. Help me to recognize and encourage them, lifting them up in prayer and offering support as they serve You. Amen.

CHALLENGE
Identify someone in your church or community who serves faithfully but quietly. Take a moment this week to thank them personally and let them know how their work blesses others.

DAY 2: HONORING FELLOW WORKERS

Scripture Reading: Romans 16:3-4
Focus Verse: "Greet Priscilla and Aquila, my co-workers in Christ Jesus. They risked their lives for me. Not only I but all the churches of the Gentiles are grateful to them."

DEVOTION

Paul's mention of Priscilla and Aquila in Romans 16:3-4 highlights the importance of honoring those who work tirelessly for the gospel. This couple, described as Paul's co-workers, risked their lives for the sake of Christ and supported the early church in profound ways. Their dedication serves as a powerful example of faithfulness and courage.

Honoring fellow workers isn't just about recognition—it's about showing gratitude for their sacrifice and partnership in ministry. Priscilla and Aquila weren't just close to Paul; they played a significant role in supporting the growth of the church and spreading the gospel.

Consider Mark and Lydia, a couple in their congregation known for hosting small groups and mentoring young couples. They often went above and beyond to create a welcoming space for spiritual growth. When their pastor publicly thanked them during a service, it encouraged them to keep serving faithfully.

Honoring fellow workers doesn't diminish our own contributions; it strengthens the body of Christ by acknowledging the unique roles God has given each person. When we express gratitude for others' labor, we glorify God and build a culture of mutual encouragement.

As you reflect on those who labor alongside you in ministry, take time to pray for them, encourage them, and thank them. Your words and actions can uplift their spirits and remind them of the eternal value of their work.

FURTHER READING:
1 Thessalonians 5:12-13; Philippians 1:3-5

PRAYER
Lord, thank You for the co-workers You've placed in my life. Teach me to honor and encourage them, recognizing their faithfulness and sacrifice. Help me to serve alongside them with humility and love. Amen.

CHALLENGE
Reach out to someone who serves in your church or ministry. Write them a note of appreciation, pray for them, or offer practical help as a way to honor their work.

DAY 3: RECOGNIZING HARD WORK

Scripture Reading: Romans 16:6
Focus Verse: "Greet Mary, who worked very hard for you."

DEVOTION

Paul's simple yet profound acknowledgment of Mary in Romans 16:6 reminds us of the importance of recognizing hard work in the service of the Lord. Though we know little about Mary's specific contributions, her labor for the church was significant enough for Paul to highlight it, demonstrating the value of her dedication.

Serving in ministry often involves unseen sacrifices—long hours, emotional investment, and steadfast perseverance. Paul's recognition of Mary encourages us to notice and appreciate those who work diligently behind the scenes. These faithful servants strengthen the church in ways that may not always be visible but are essential to its growth and mission.

Consider Kevin, a member of the church maintenance team who ensured everything was prepared for Sunday services. Though few people noticed his efforts, his pastor made it a point to thank him during a staff meeting. Kevin's work became a testimony of faithfulness, inspiring others to take their roles seriously.

Recognizing hard work is not about seeking praise or promoting individuals; it's about glorifying God for how He uses His people to accomplish His purposes. When we acknowledge someone's efforts, we affirm their role in God's plan and encourage them to continue serving with joy.

Take time this week to reflect on the contributions of those around you. Whether their efforts are large or small, visible or hidden, their work matters to God and to the body of Christ.

FURTHER READING:

Colossians 3:23-24; 1 Corinthians 15:58

PRAYER

Lord, thank You for the hard work of those who serve Your church. Teach me to recognize and encourage their efforts, lifting them up in prayer and gratitude. Help me to labor faithfully for Your glory. Amen.

CHALLENGE

Think of someone whose hard work has blessed your church or community. Take a moment this week to thank them personally or through a note of appreciation.

DAY 4: BROTHERS AND SISTERS IN CHRIST

Scripture Reading: Romans 16:7-10

Focus Verse: "Greet Andronicus and Junia, my fellow Jews who have been in prison with me. They are outstanding among the apostles, and they were in Christ before I was."

DEVOTION

Paul's greetings in Romans 16:7-10 reflect the deep relationships he shared with his brothers and sisters in Christ. These individuals weren't just acquaintances—they were fellow laborers, friends, and spiritual family. Their faithfulness in ministry, even in suffering, shows the strength of the bond we have as believers.

Being part of the body of Christ means more than attending church services; it means sharing life with one another. Paul's mention of Andronicus, Junia, and others reminds us of the importance of honoring and supporting one another, celebrating both their faith and their sacrifices.

John, a missionary in a remote region, often relied on the encouragement of letters and prayers from his church family. Though miles away, their partnership strengthened his faith and reminded him of the global fellowship of believers. Like Paul's recognition of his co-laborers, their support was a lifeline.

Brothers and sisters in Christ are gifts from God, given to encourage, challenge, and walk alongside us in our faith journey. Their presence reminds us that we are not alone and that together, we reflect the love and unity of God's family.

Take time this week to reflect on the relationships you have with fellow believers. How can you honor and encourage them in their walk with Christ?

FURTHER READING:

Galatians 6:10; 1 Corinthians 12:26-27

PRAYER

Lord, thank You for the gift of my brothers and sisters in Christ. Teach me to honor and support them in love, recognizing the unique roles they play in Your kingdom. Help me to walk in unity and fellowship with them. Amen.

CHALLENGE

Reach out to a brother or sister in Christ this week. Offer words of encouragement, pray with them, or thank them for their faithfulness in the Lord.

DAY 5: WELCOMING ONE ANOTHER IN LOVE

Scripture Reading: Romans 16:11-13
Focus Verse: "Greet Rufus, chosen in the Lord, and his mother, who has been a mother to me, too."

DEVOTION

Paul's personal greeting in Romans 16:11-13 highlights the warmth and depth of relationships within the body of Christ. Rufus and his mother weren't just acquaintances to Paul—they were part of his spiritual family. Rufus's mother's care for Paul demonstrated the love and hospitality that should characterize Christian fellowship.

Welcoming one another in love goes beyond formal greetings. It means opening our hearts and lives to others, treating them as family in Christ. This kind of hospitality reflects God's love and creates a space where faith can flourish.

Consider Anna, who hosted weekly Bible studies in her home. Her willingness to welcome newcomers and provide a warm environment helped many feel connected to the church and strengthened their faith. Her simple acts of love mirrored the motherly care Paul described in his letter.

Welcoming others isn't limited to our homes; it's about creating an atmosphere of love and acceptance wherever we go. When we greet one another with genuine care and hospitality, we reflect the heart of God, who welcomes all who come to Him.

Take time this week to think about how you can extend this kind of love to someone in your community. Your actions may be the encouragement they need to feel valued and supported in their faith.

FURTHER READING:

1 Peter 4:9; Hebrews 13:1-2

PRAYER

Lord, thank You for welcoming me into Your family. Teach me to extend the same love and hospitality to others, creating a space where Your grace is evident. Help me to reflect Your heart in my relationships. Amen.

CHALLENGE

Identify someone in your church or community who might feel overlooked or disconnected. Make a point to greet them warmly, invite them to join you in fellowship, or offer them a small act of kindness.

DAY 6: UNITY AND VIGILANCE

Scripture Reading: Romans 16:17-18
Focus Verse: "I urge you, brothers and sisters, to
watch out for those who cause divisions and put obstacles in your way that are contrary to the teaching you have learned. Keep away from them."

DEVOTION

Unity within the body of Christ is precious, but it must be protected
with vigilance. In Romans 16:17-18, Paul warns believers to be watchful
of those who cause divisions or promote false teachings. Maintaining
unity requires both love and discernment.

Paul's words remind us that division often stems from selfish motives, such as personal ambition or the desire for power. These actions
not only harm relationships but also weaken the church's witness to the
world. As followers of Christ, we are called to seek unity and avoid anything that disrupts it.

Consider Michael, who noticed growing tension in his small group
due to a member's divisive comments. Instead of ignoring the issue, Michael gently addressed the concerns and reminded the group of their
shared purpose in Christ. His willingness to confront the problem with
grace helped restore harmony.

Unity doesn't mean ignoring truth or tolerating harmful behavior.
It means prioritizing God's word and working together to build a strong
and loving community. By staying vigilant and rooted in Scripture, we
protect the church from division and ensure it remains focused on Christ.

Take time this week to reflect on your role in fostering unity. Are
there areas where vigilance or discernment is needed? Seek God's guidance in protecting and strengthening the body of Christ.

FURTHER READING:
Ephesians 4:3; Titus 3:9-10

PRAYER
Lord, thank You for the gift of unity in the body of Christ. Teach me to be vigilant in protecting it and to confront division with grace and love. Help me to foster harmony that glorifies You. Amen.

CHALLENGE
Reflect on your words and actions this week. Are they contributing to unity in your church or community? If needed, take steps to resolve conflict or encourage others toward harmony.

DAY 7: GLORY TO GOD THROUGH CHRIST

Scripture Reading: Romans 16:25-27
Focus Verse: "To the only wise God be glory forever through Jesus Christ! Amen."

DEVOTION

Paul concludes his letter to the Romans with a beautiful doxology, directing all glory to God. In Romans 16:25-27, he praises God for His wisdom, power, and grace revealed through Jesus Christ. This closing reminds us that everything in our lives and ministry should point to God's glory.

Glorifying God means recognizing His greatness in all things. It's about living in awe of His redemptive plan and allowing His Spirit to transform every aspect of our lives. When we glorify God, we align our hearts with His purposes and reflect His light to the world.

Consider Rachel, who kept a gratitude journal as part of her daily routine. Each night, she wrote down ways she saw God's glory in her life—from answered prayers to the beauty of creation. This practice deepened her faith and reminded her of God's constant presence.

Paul's doxology also highlights the role of Jesus Christ in bringing glory to God. Through His life, death, and resurrection, Jesus revealed God's character and made a way for us to live in relationship with Him. Our lives, in turn, should be a reflection of that same glory.

Take time this week to reflect on how your life glorifies God. Whether through worship, service, or simple acts of love, let everything you do point to His greatness.

FURTHER READING:

Psalm 115:1; 1 Corinthians 10:31

PRAYER

Lord, to You alone be the glory forever. Teach me to live in a way that honors and reflects Your greatness. Let my life be a testimony of Your wisdom and love through Jesus Christ. Amen.

CHALLENGE

Spend time in worship this week, focusing solely on God's glory. Reflect on ways you can point others to His greatness through your actions and words

WALKING FURTHER:
WEEK 20 QUESTIONS

1. How can you encourage faithful servants in your church as Paul did with Phoebe?

2. What can you learn from Paul's example of honoring his fellow workers in Christ?

3. Why is recognizing hard work important for building up the church?

4. What steps can you take to treat your church community as true brothers and sisters in Christ?

5. How can you be more welcoming to new or unfamiliar faces in your church?

6. What does it mean to be vigilant about unity in your fellowship? How can you protect it?

7. Reflect on how your life brings glory to God. What specific area can you dedicate to His glory this week?

PERSONAL REFLECTION ON THE ROMANS ROAD

As you come to the end of *The Romans Road*, I invite you to take a moment to reflect on the journey you've just completed. Romans is more than just a book of doctrine; it's a letter filled with the heartbeat of the gospel—the transformative power of God's grace and love for each of us.

Through each devotional, you've uncovered the depth of God's love, the seriousness of sin, the gift of salvation, and the beauty of a new life in Christ. You've been reminded that God's grace is sufficient, His promises are unshakable, and His purpose for you is eternal. As you look back over the chapters, consider the ways these truths have touched your life, shaped your understanding, and deepened your relationship with God.

What stood out to you the most? Was it the reminder that we are justified by faith, the call to live a transformed life, or the assurance that nothing can separate us from God's love? Each verse and truth we've explored together is an invitation to live more fully in God's grace, sharing His love with those around us.

Take time to ask God to seal these truths in your heart. Allow His Spirit to continue to guide and teach you, bringing fresh insights as you meditate on His Word. May *The Romans Road* not be an end but a foundation—a place from which you can grow deeper in faith, stronger in hope, and more equipped to share the gospel with others.

As you move forward I encourage you to revisit Romans whenever you need a reminder of God's unending grace and transformative power. Let this journey be a stepping stone, one that draws you closer to the heart of God and fills you with confidence in His promises.

Thank you for taking this journey. May God bless you richly as you continue walking in His grace and truth.

In Christ's love and service,
Dr. Ralph Jenkins

Jehovah Jireh Ministries
To learn more about our ministry go to:
www.jehovahjirehministries.com

INVITATION TO CONTINUE WITH
FOUNDATIONS OF FAITH

Dear Reader,

Congratulations on completing *The Romans Road*! You've taken a deep dive into the heart of Paul's teachings, uncovering life-transforming truths about salvation, faith, and God's love. But there's so much more to discover on your journey of faith!

If you'd like to go further, I invite you to continue with *Foundations of Faith*. This devotional will walk you through the essential doctrines of the Christian faith, exploring core beliefs that equip and encourage new and seasoned believers alike. Through daily readings, practical applications, and reflections, *Foundations of Faith* will help you grow stronger in your relationship with God, giving you a solid base for a life of purpose and trust in Him.

Join me in building upon the foundation you've already established through *The Romans Road*. Let's continue this journey together, one day at a time, as we deepen our understanding of what it means to walk by faith and live out God's calling.

Thank you for your commitment to growing in the Lord. May this next step be filled with encouragement, discovery, and strength in Him!

In Christ's love,

INVITATION TO
CONTINUE WITH
REVELATION UNVEILED

Dear Reader,

You've just completed an incredible journey through *The Romans Road*, and I commend you for your dedication and heart for God's word! Now that you've experienced the riches of Romans, I'd like to invite you to take another step forward by exploring *Revelation Unveiled*.

Revelation Unveiled is designed to bring clarity and encouragement as we uncover God's ultimate plan for the future. This devotional will guide you through the prophecies and promises found in Revelation, helping you understand what was, what is, and what is to come. Through daily readings, reflections, and practical applications, you'll gain insight into God's sovereignty, the hope of Christ's return, and the purpose He has for us as we await His glorious coming.

This journey through Revelation isn't just about understanding prophecy—it's about strengthening your faith, equipping you with hope, and empowering you to live boldly for Christ in these times. I invite you to join me as we dive deeper into the awe-inspiring visions and messages of this powerful book, allowing God's promises to speak life, hope, and purpose into every part of our lives.

Thank you for your commitment to knowing God more deeply. May *Revelation Unveiled* bless you abundantly as we look forward to His coming with joy and anticipation!

In Christ's hope,

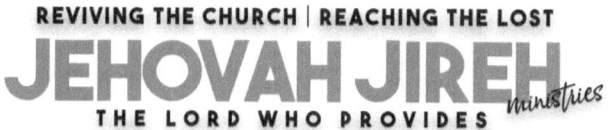

Founded in 2019 by Dr. Ralph and Tammy Jenkins, Jehovah Jireh Ministries exists to bring the gospel to people groups around the world.

We have a deep burden to share the Gospel of Christ with the world and disciple those saints who do not have readily available the resources or pastors to help build their faith in Christ.

Our mission focuses on planting churches, training pastors, and holding revivals and crusades wherever God leads us, and disciple believers. Currently, much of our work is concentrated in India and Pakistan, where we have witnessed almost 30,000 people come to Christ since the ministry began.

Jehovah Jireh Ministries operates prayer and conference centers in both India and Pakistan, where we equip national pastors to preach the gospel and shepherd their congregations.

In addition, we operate a small Children's Home in India, meeting children's physical needs while teaching them the Word of God. We are currently working to build a new children's home in India and to expand this mission into Pakistan with a children's home for 100 children. God has opened remarkable doors, allowing us to reach the "least of these" with the love of Christ.

Beyond our work in India and Pakistan, we partner with the Roma (Gypsy) people in Romania and are prayerfully establishing a ministry presence in the UK.

The needs are immense, but we trust that the Lord will provide for all He has called us to do. As Mark 16:15 says, *"And He said to them, 'Go into all the world and preach the gospel to all creation.'"* Wherever He leads, we will follow.

By purchasing our devotionals, you are hopefully being blessed spiritually. You are also supporting the mission of Jehovah Jireh Ministries. Your contribution helps us bring the gospel to the nations, and for that, we—and our Board of Directors—are humbled and grateful.

Until He Comes, We Must Go,
Dr. Ralph W Jenkins
Founder & CEO

To learn more about us, please visit www.jehovahjirehministries.com

www.ingramcontent.com/pod-product-compliance
Lightning Source LLC
Chambersburg PA
CBHW030356130626
46549CB00004B/1512